Why Evolution is a Fraud:

A Secular and Common-Sense Deconstruction

Why Evolution is a Fraud:

A Secular and Common-Sense Deconstruction

Copyright © 2007 by Tom Sutcliff.

Red State Publishing, Inc.

ISBN: 978-0-6151-4058-2

1. Current Issues
2. Politics/Culture
3. History, American
4. History, European
5. Evolution

TABLE OF CONTENTS

1. Why it Matters 1
2. Adaptation, Not Evolution 9
3. Delusion and Distortion 21
4. Racist Roots Bear Poisonous Fruits 35
5. How Genetics Disproves Evolution 61
6. Mathematically Impossible 73
7. Similarity Does Not Equal Ancestry 91
8. Agendascience 103
Acknowledgments 121
About the Author 123
Notes 125
Bibliography 135
Index 145

Evofraud.com

Introduction

"Imagination and rationalization are no substitute for the truth"

Anonymous

Evolution—the idea that time and random mutations turned molecules into mathematicians—is a scientific fraud. Unlike chemistry, physics and biology, Darwinian evolution is a pseudo-scientific philosophy that demands far more faith than any religion the world has ever known.

The mythology of evolution, passed down as fact rather than theory, is the default position of many scientists. While these scientists may be experts in their chosen field, they have chosen not to challenge the religion of evolution for fear of being demonized by prominent evolutionists and a much-too-gullible media.

Why Evolution is a Fraud

Instead of using the scientific method of making a hypothesis and using experiments to prove or disprove it, evolutionists must start from a fractured foundation and rationalize elements of biology, chemistry and genetics into supporting their phony conclusions. Biochemistry, physics and mathematics contribute to the undeniable fact that evolution is an idea that's better suited for philosophy than science.

In writing *Why Evolution is a Fraud*, I approached this subject from the standpoint of how well evolution fared on its own—without attacking or advocating a differing view. Forcing evolution to stand on its own is the purpose of this book. By the end, you'll know why evolution cannot stand up unless it is attacking something else.

The ideas in this book are accessible to most anyone. You don't have to have a bunch of degrees after your name or papers published in scholarly journals to understand why evolution is a fraud. In fact, as you read this book and absorb media information about the evolutionary debate, one thing will jump out at you: Evolutionists harshly demonize those who dare to question the "validity" of evolution. Why? Evolution does not have the facts on its side.

Introduction

Evoligion—the religion of evolution—accurately describes the irrational, anti-scientific worship of a fraud that evolutionists proclaim as the truth. The amount of faith required to believe in evolution is more than any theistic faith could possibly demand. While adaptation is something that Darwin was right about when he observed the finches of the Galapagos, the term evolution has been used to justify the unscientific and the absurd. This is abundantly described in the chapter called 'Mathematically Impossible.'

The chapter 'Similarity Does Not Equal Ancestry' mercilessly hammers the supposed fossil evidence that evolutionists so gleefully use to validate their findings. Speaking of similarity, you'll uncover the racist evolutionary view that suggests that some humans were closer to apes because they were not white. The under-reported and undeniable history continues to this day as the framework for evolution. By the end of this book, you'll wonder why anyone ever believed in evolution.

Why It Matters
Chapter 1

"If you don't stand for anything, anything goes"

Radio talk show host and author Dennis Prager, May 17th, 2006

The acceptance and normalization of evolution addresses a much larger issue than science. Evolution supposely explains the reason for our existence. The "free-thinking" evolutionists believe that we are simply the result of a cosmic collision of biochemistry and chance. This scientifically-invalid position is alluring to those who reject existence of God because it means that there is no objective, moral truth. To the evolutionist, values are as fluid as one's emotions and animal urges. Since they claim that we are just advanced apes derived from a common ancestor, this simply helps increase the speed at which our society slips into decline.

Far from being an avalanche of cultural change into atheism, evolution took decades to change the world. While Charles Darwin's landmark book *The Origin of Species by Means of Natural Selection, or, the Preservation of Favored Races in the Struggle for Life* was a hit when it came out in 1859, the change didn't happen overnight. Darwin's ground-breaking book helped spawn disciples who passionately advocated the idea that humans are just highly-evolved apes. Thomas Huxley was one of those people. He crusaded against the anti-evolutionists like a man possessed. His unshakeable adherence to evolution was unparalled.

Assigning ape status to the politically powerless in the 1860s was easy. Those of dark skin, whose ancestors came from Africa or Aboriginal Australia, became convenient scapegoats in the evolutionary quest to replace God with man. As you'll see in the chapter titled 'Racist Roots Bear Poisonous Fruits,' the consequences of decades of evolutionary thought helped pave the way for some of the most horrific atrocities in the history of mankind.

The alleged scientific status of evolution made it easier to accept in the age of scientific enlightenment. In

Why It Matters

the previous 200 years to Darwin's 1859 publication of *The Origin of Species*, scientists such as Newton and Watt blazed permanent trails that we walk upon to this day. Their contributions to physics are many. The term 'Newton' and 'Watt' are used to describe units of energy.[1]

I suspect that people like Thomas Huxley were eager to grab the brass ring of biology, much like Newton did for physics. What was biology's contribution to the scientific enlightenment? In *Darwin, Marx, Wagner: Critique of a Heritage*, author Jacques Barzun shows how Darwin and *The Origin of Species* filled that void by naming one of his chapters 'The Newton of Biology.'[2] However, Darwin's findings in *The Origin of Species* show adaptation, not evolution. Specifically, the changes of the finch bird beaks on the Galapagos Islands are excellent examples of what Darwin got right—adaptation.

The birds needed to adapt so they could get food and survive. Over generations, this did happen and adaptations have been proven again and again to be scientific fact. From the cross breeding of various plants by Mendel in the early 19th century to the genetic engineering of today, adaptation is an unquestionable fact.

However, evolution is not adaptation. As much as the term 'evolution' is so casually tossed about when people refer to adaptation, it does not have the scientific validity that adaptation does. You'll understand why in the upcoming chapter titled 'Adaptation, Not Evolution.'

Nonetheless, the defenders of Darwinian thought counter that humans and apes have a 'common ancestor.' According to them, we have evolved from some kind of ape-like hominid that is conveniently absent—just like the supposed proof in the fossil record. The implication of evolution is that humans are just a level or two above monkeys. While I freely admit that some people act like animals, they, and the rest of humanity, do not have a common ancestor with apes.

Now, let's fast forward to the 20th century. The saying "If it feels good, do it," was the 1960s counter-culture catchphrase for breaking the shackles of "backward" rules, "outdated" morals and objective truth. This helped legitimize the idea that feelings are more important than standards. While this standard might easily be the credo of apes, gorillas and countless other animals, it does not work for humans. How we feel toward an issue should not cloud objective and factual truth. To paraphrase a famous quote, we all have the right to our own opinions, but we don't have the right to our own facts.

In addition to Huxley, the intellectuals of the Vienna, Austria accepted evolution and began to spread it more and more. Viennese newspapers in the last 40 years of the 19th century showed strong advocacy of evolution and its inescapable partner, atheism.[3]

At the same time, people like Friedrich Nietzsche took hold of evolution and expanded on it. "God is dead," is the 3-word trademark that we attribute to the militantly atheistic Nietzsche. Not surprisingly, Nietzsche believed in moral relativism. "There are no facts, only interpretations," Nietzsche said.[4] Sounds like political correctness 100 years ahead of its time. As Nietzsche's anti-morality became more common in Vienna, it helped normalize the idea that evolution was true.

In a chilling prediction of the horrors to come, Nietzsche believed that Darwinism's results would happen through war, eugenics and racial extermination.[5] "Nietzsche's philosophy had much influence everywhere, but especially in his native Germany, where it contributed to the growth of German militarism."

Richard Weikart's excellent book *From Darwin to Hitler: Evolution Ethics, Eugenics, and Racism in Germany*, exposes the moral bankruptcy that followed evolution. "If morality was built on social instincts that changed over evolutionary time, then morality must be relative to the conditions of life at any given time. Darwinism...contributed to the rise of moral relativism." [6]

Weikart shows how the merge of atheism and Darwinism helped reframe views on human life. "Darwinism also contributed to a rethinking of the value of human life in the late nineteenth century. In order to make human evolution plausible, prominent Darwinists argued that humans were not qualitatively different from animals. Also, the significant of the individual life did not seem all that great considering the mass death brought on by the Darwinian struggle for existence." [7]

Evolution advocates the idea humans are just advanced animals and that the human being is the ultimate authority. Subsequently, it becomes easy—almost mandatory—to discard concepts like God, morals and objective truth. Why obey 'ancient' standards when science

Why It Matters

has proven that you are just a sophisticated simian?

Notice the parallel of those who adamantly endorse evolution and their raging hatred for any kind of theistic belief system. Most, in my estimation, are atheists who are proud to crow that faith is just opium for the masses. Nowhere is this view more strongly held than in the realm of academia. The modern day evolutionary brainiacs like Niles Eldridge, for example, view faith as a disease to be extracted from the weak-minded simpletons and replaced with the religion of evolution.

People are free to believe as they choose. I certainly do not advocate the banning of evolution. If people want to believe that ape-like creatures turned into astrophysicists, I won't stop them. Just as I won't stop them from believing that the earth is flat. In fact, evolution is the modern-day flat-earth doctrine. Why? Evolutionary thought says that if something is similar to you, it must be your ancestor. If a bone structure or a DNA reading shows similarities, evolutionary thought says that similarity equals ancestry.

By extension, the flat-earth crowd of centuries past believed that if you sailed too far, you'd fall off the edge of the earth. They based this on what they could see with their own eyes, and not on reasoned analytical thought. The concept of gravitational pull had not been fully understood and explained yet.

An example is a glass of water. If you tilt it, it moves to a level position in the glass. If you tilt the edge of the glass so that it's parallel to the ground, the water falls out. Evolution uses the same mindset. If you find a fossil that vaguely resembles a human being, it must be a distant ancestor. If you go to the zoo and see ape mothers tending to their babies like a human mother would, the apes must represent part of our family tree.

Like the flat-earthers who knew nothing of gravitational pull and the laws of physics, evolutionists demand that we break the most basic laws of probability. Furthermore, evolution requires us to discard the ever-advancing work in genetics, which shows the intricate programming code of life. This will become clear in the chapter called 'How Genetics Disproves Evolution.'

Adaptation, Not Evolution
Chapter 2

> "There are few nudities so objectionable as the naked truth."
>
> American essayist
> Agnes Repplier (1858–1950)

According to evolutionists, natural selection is the process where living organisms develop changes over many generations. The negative changes hurt the organism and the positive changes help it. Evolution, according to its advocates, is the sum total of these positive changes that allow an organism to cross over into another species. An example is the idea that birds evolved from reptiles.

While adaptation does happen, evolution does not. Darwin was right about this and he demonstrated it in his observations of the Galapagos Island finches. Over successive generations, the beaks of the finches adapted to environmental changes. For instance, the finch beaks became narrower to reach food in narrow spots.

While adaptations within a species do happen, the idea of an animal jumping the species fence has no basis in scientific fact. But what about the fossil record? Doesn't it show that evolution is true? No. Contrary to what the mainstream media and the academic elites often shout, the fossil record does not back up their claims that evolution is a proven scientific fact. The opposite is true.

"Darwin had an excuse. In his day fossil finds were relatively scarce. Today...we have an abundance of fossils. Still, we have yet to find even one legitimate transition from one species to another," according to author and radio talk show host Hank Hanegraaff's book *The FACE That Demonstrates the Farce of Evolution*. The British Museum of Natural History has sixty million fossils but, according to the museum's senior paleontologist Colin Patterson, no verifiable transitions from one species to another have been found. "His statement underscores the fact that the fossil record is an embarrassment to evolutionists," writes Hanegraaff.[1]

Joe White and Nicholas Comninellis reinforce this point in their book *Darwin's Demise: Why Evolution Can't Take the Heat*. "The fossils once thought to be human ancestors are now known to be only those of extinct apes." Dr. Wolfgang Smith states in the book that "on the fundamental level, it becomes a rigorously demonstrable fact that there are no transitional types, and that the so-called missing links are indeed non-existent."[2]

But things like facts don't matter when you are trying to deify yourself and catapult your area of study into legitimate science. Simply rationalize adaptations, add millions of years and claim that similarity equals ancestry. We'll go into more detail in later chapters, but evolution's history is littered with blatant hoaxes that were made to make this pseudoscience seem legitimate.

So Darwin used the term 'Natural Selection' instead, thus putting the evolutionary forces of nature in command. And since the evolutionists believe themselves to be the ultimate authority on nature, evolution (aka Natural Selection) has replaced God. This God-replacement paradigm got a cataclysmic boost in 1859 when Darwin published *The Origin of Species*.

However, what Darwin showed was adaptation, not evolution. In his observations of the finches of the Galapagos Islands, Darwin did show that successive generations of birds adapted their beaks to get food. This is an excellent example of an adaptation that allowed an animal to survive.

Speaking of things needing to survive, the old tale about the Birmingham Moths is a myth that evolutionists like to keep alive. The story goes like this: In the mid 19th century, increasing amounts of black soot from the newly-established local factories darkened the tree trunks that the moths called home. This increase in contrast made the moths easier to become a predator's meal. To counter this, the moths became darker and darker over successive generations. This prevented their numbers from nearing extinction by hungry birds.

The problem with this story is that moths do not live on tree trunks. Another problem is that even if the moths did change color, it would only be proof of adaptation because there is no species transition.

Yet countless biology textbooks over the last four decades have carried the famous picture of the light and dark-colored moths. "The pictures in the textbooks are now known to be fakes. They are pictures of dead moths glued to a tree," according to an article titled 'Horses and

Adaptation, Not Evolution

Peppered Moths' at <u>ScienceAgainstEvolution.org</u>.

"The reason they could not get a good picture of live moths on tree trunks had nothing to do with lighting, or the tendency of moths not to stay put very long. They could not get a good picture of live peppered moths on tree trunks because peppered moths don't normally land on tree trunks. They rest on the undersides of leaves. That's why there was a scandal about the photographs. The pictures weren't recreations of situations that really occur in nature. They were fraudulent representations of something that rarely, if ever, happens."[3]

The photos, taken in the mid 1950s by British physician H.B.D. Kettlewell, were supposed to show evolution in action. "Kettlewell's ambitions would exceed the strength of his science," wrote Judith Hooper in the book *Of Moths and Men: the Untold Story of Science and the Peppered Moth.*[4] "He wanted—needed—to prove that the moths were evolving to a darker color in response to industrial pollution, for this would put the finishing touches on Darwin's theory." Exactly! Hooper nails the agenda-science that I'll get into later in the book.

In addition to this, a respected British peppered moth researcher named Sir Cyril Clarke wrote in a paper that "all we have observed is where the moths do not spend the day. In 25 years we have only found two betularia [moths] on the tree trunks or walls adjacent to our traps," according to Hooper's book.[5] Clarke was also a close friend of Kettlewell's.

Darwinists believe that evolution is the sum total of many adaptations. By evolutionary reasoning, the beaks of those Galapagos finches could have been the most recent development of an animal that evolved over millions of years from a reptile. Chance, adaptations and time engineered reptile scales into flight-worthy feathers, according to the mathematics of evolution. However, real sciences, like chemistry and physics, use precise mathematics. Evolutionary math requires faith instead of facts and lies instead of truth.

But evolutionists counter that mutations could account for the transition from one species to another. Mutations! Maybe evolutionists need to get out more, but I'll break the news right here: mutations are negative things. If someone calls you a 'mutant,' rest assured that it's an insult.

Adaptation, Not Evolution

To further clarify the point, simply turn on your TV. The show *The Simpsons* has a recurring mutant character—a three-eyed fish that periodically surfaces in the toxic lake behind the nuclear power plant where Homer works. But I suppose that the obvious satire is lost on our highly-evolved friends, since they love to sport those stupid walking fish emblems on their cars.

The problem with mutations is that they are almost always detrimental to the organism. In a section on chromosomal abnormalities, the *DK Ultimate Dictionary of Science* show that on a human "X" sex chromosome, mutations in certain spots result in cleft palates, hemophilia, skin diseases and color blindness.[6]

Amazingly, evolutionists would have us believe that random mutations could have created something as highly engineered as feathered wings from reptilian scales. As Hanegraaff explains in his book *The Face that Demonstrates the Farce of Evolution*, the meticulous engineering of flight-worthy feathers excludes the idea that random chance (natural selection) made them from mutations. "The central shaft of a feather has a series of barbs projecting from each side at right angles. Rows of smaller barbules in turn protrude from both sides of the barb. Tiny hooks, called barbicels, project downward from one side of the adjacent barbules. In some feathers there may be as many as a million barbules cooperating to bind the barbs into a complete feather, impervious to air penetration." [7]

Now that we've established the fact that mutations do not improve organisms, it's important to understand basic genetics. Parent organisms—whether they are humans or lizards—pass genetic material to their offspring for the creation of the same kind of organism. Humans don't give birth to lizards. I realize that this is common sense, but evolutionary thought requires us to abandon rational thought.

Evolution also requires us to suspend mathematical probability and believe that simple organisms turned into complex ones. While I'll provide examples in the latter chapter called 'Mathematically Impossible,' I can safely say that systems, left to their own devices, do not become more intelligent, more ordered and more organized. This is another nugget of common sense that evolutionary thought discards.

Evolutionists counter that changes are not random

but shaped by the environment which surrounds the organism. Organisms do adapt to their environment but no amount of mutations and variations over successive generations will cause a reptile to turn into a bird.

Hanegraaff, poses the issue this way: "...air friction acting on genetic mutation supposedly frayed the outer edges of reptilian scales. Thus, in the course of millions of years, scales became more and more like feathers until, one day, the perfect feather emerged. To say the least, this idea must stretch the credulity of even the most ardent evolutionists."[8]

Yet evolutionists use this absurd logic to justify the existence of a supposed link between reptiles and birds called Archaeopteryx. Phonysaurus Maximus might be a better name for this imaginary link, since Archaeopteryx is 100% bird and 0% reptile. The journal *Science* slams the door on this flying reptile fantasy by stating that "Archaeopteryx probably cannot tell us much about the early origin of feathers and flight in true protobirds because Archaeopteryx was, in a modern sense, a bird."[9] *Darwin's Demise* cites a quote that sums this controversy up nicely: "Paleontologists have tried to turn

Archaeopteryx into an earth-bound, feathered dinosaur. But it's not. It's a bird, a perching bird. And no amount of 'paleobabble' is going to change that." [10]

In a June 18th, 2002 ScientificAmerican.com article by John Rennie about evolution, the author admits that speciation—one species evolving into another—is rare. This is the one encouraging bit of intellectual honesty to come from the evolutionary camp because the process of evolution requires us to believe that a single-celled organism turned into a modern human being.

For evolution to be a legitimate process, it would have to be extremely common. Furthermore, if it was that common you'd find countless examples in the fossil record, as Darwin suggested. But now we have more fossils available and far more research on the process of evolution but we are not one step closer to finding one valid example of speciation.

Hanegraaff points out the embarrassment of the fossil record in the chapter 'Fossil Follies' where he cites the words of Colin Patterson, senior paleontologist at the British Museum of Natural History, which holds the world's largest collection of fossil specimens. "If I knew of

Adaptation, Not Evolution

any [evolutionary transitions], fossil or living, I would certainly have included them [in my book *Evolution*]."[11]

Adaptation can account for changes in a bird's beak, but it is a huge stretch of logic to say speciation—which an ardent evolutionist has admitted is rare—caused something like flight-worthy bird feathers to develop from reptile scales. But evolutionists have a long history of rationalizing information to fit their atheistic agenda. The Darwinian term 'survival of the fittest' is an example.

Survival of the fittest is a term that you'd think would be self-explanatory—that the 'fittest' survive. Not so according to James Trefil, author of *1001 Things Everyone Should Know About Science*. He states that "Darwin himself used this phrase, but it is often misrepresented or misunderstood. Darwin used the term 'fit' to describe individuals who are successful in producing offspring in the next generation, nothing more."[12]

Then why call it survival of the fittest? Darwin spent two decades working on *The Origin of Species* after his trip to the Galapagos, so I doubt that he simply meant this term to mean superior reproduction.

Another problem with evolution is the idea the one

animal needed to survive more than another animal. For instance, a bird that could catch prey faster than competitor birds would be more likely to survive. Over the generations, the slow birds would become extinct because they could not feed and reproduce. This means that the survivors would be the fast birds, which reproduced other fast birds.

But weak and slow organisms continue to exist. The circular reasoning of survival of the fittest does not work. In human beings, we still have birth defects and genetic disorders that continue over the generations.

Evolutionists counter that this is just part of the constant evolutionary battle, where other organisms like mutating genes battle for survival, thus perpetuating birth defects. But this reasoning counters the survival of the fittest doctrine. If you still have birth defects, you do not have a 'fit' group of organisms. So survival of the fittest collapses like a house of cards.

But who needs sound reasoning and critical thinking when you are pushing a pseudoscience like evolution.

Delusion and Distortion
Chapter 3

"A lie told often enough becomes the truth"

Russian revolutionary and founder of Bolshevism, Vladimir Lenin (1870–1924)

Evolution's best defense is a blitzkrieg of bigotry toward those who reject the hominid-to-man theory. Its defenders must demonize anti-evolutionists as illiterate, Bible-thumping hayseeds who are just not smart enough to realize that science has replaced God.

Some evolutionists claim that teaching evolution is essential to our ability to compete in the increasingly high-tech globalized market. This idea has to be the pinnacle of evolutionary absurdity, and that's quite an accomplishment for a "science" that has almost no demand in the marketplace and no verifiable facts. I say 'almost no demand' because there are, and there will continue to be, academic elites who will never let go of their irrational evoligion, regardless of how much science proves them wrong.

While it is true that globalization is making our world smaller and the demand for high-tech knowledge and problem-solving skills is increasing, evolution is the antithesis of a high-tech, market-driven science. Real sciences can, and do, stand on their own without absurd theories and a history of hoaxes. While real science learns from its failures, evolution requires us to believe in failure.

Unfortunately for Darwinism, more and more people are demanding that evolution adhere to scientific standards. The days of evolution being accepted as scientific fact are over because when you force evolution to stand on its own—without attacking something else—it collapses like a house of cards.

We all know that to compete in the globalized, high-tech world market, students must be proficient in disciplines like computer programming, chemistry, physics and mathematics. Engineers who help make our world run more effectively and efficiently did not get there because they learned the intricacies of evolutionary thought. They

Delusion and Distortion

spent years studying advanced mathematics, physics and chemistry so they'd have a foundation for designing skyscrapers that don't collapse like Darwin's house of cards. The same holds true of physicians, who undergo grueling and rigorous coursework that covers the complex mechanics of the human body. In addition to the demanding coursework, both fields require aspiring engineers and physicians to pass licensing exams. This helps ensure that our society can reasonably trust them to do their jobs according to solid scientific principles.

But when it comes to evolution, there is nothing legitimate or scientific about it. Darwinian thought is just an atheistic philosophy masquerading as science. Its history is littered with blatant frauds like Piltdown man, Java man, Nebraska man and others that I'll explain further in the chapter called 'Similarity Does not Equal Ancestry.'

In light of the increased erosion of evolution's credibility and non-existent fossil evidence, its defenders have to fabricate outrageous theories, like punctuated equilibrium, to advance its cause. Heavily promoted in the 1970s by Stephen Jay Gould as an alternative to the theory of gradualism, P.E. states that relatively rapid changes just happen during periods of relative calm. Poof! There it is! And this supposedly passes for science? No wonder nations like India and China are racing past the US, Canada and the UK in high-tech employment. The fact is that India and China do not have a history of advocating the scientific mythology of Darwinian evolution.

A caller on a nationally-syndicated radio talk show further illustrated the point of evolution's close mindedness. On the December 16, 2005 broadcast of *The Michael Medved Show*, the subject of Intelligent Design came up. A caller who believed in evolution stated that he objected to the mere idea of Intelligent Design because he did not want his son to have to learn another point of view. I could not believe my ears, but there it was. This caller obviously believed so strongly in evolution that he was unwilling to even consider another explanation. That's why I call it evoligion.

Science is not about pushing a philosophical agenda. It's about critical thinking and Lehigh University biochemistry professor Michael Behe delivers one of the most devastating critiques of evolution in his book

Delusion and Distortion

Darwin's Black Box. Behe demonstrates that incredibly complex natural systems like blood clotting and cell functions could not have started by random chance.

The blood clotting system that we take for granted is an amazingly complex process. As Behe describes it, "...when a person suffers a cut it ordinarily bleeds for only a short time before a clot stops the flow; the clot eventually hardens, and the cut heals over."[1] This is an active process, according to Behe, unlike what happens when the gas tank of a car is punctured. There is nothing that actively stops the leaking of gasoline from the tank.

"When a pressurized blood circulation system is punctured, clots must form quickly or the animal will bleed to death. If blood congeals at the wrong time or place, though, then the clot may block circulation as it does in heart attacks and strokes," writes Behe. "Furthermore, a clot has to slop bleeding all along the length of the cut, sealing it completely. Yet blood clotting must be confined to the cut or the entire system of the animal might solidify, killing it."[2]

Not to be dissuaded by facts, evolutionists counter that this level of precision engineering is simply the result of variations and mutations of organisms over billions of years. Specifically, trillions of changes built on trillions of other changes resulted in the complex and directional systems that, for instance, prevent us from bleeding to death. This is an example of how evolutionary thought demands that we believe the absurd and throw legitimate science out the window.

Biochemistry professor Russell Doolittle attempts to explain the blood clotting system via evolutionary process but, as Behe points out, his explanation falls short because he cannot explain why random mutations and variations over time would create this. In *Darwin's Black Box*, Behe shows that Doolittle's explanation is "...seriously inadequate because no reasons are given for the appearance of the proteins, no attempt is made to calculate the probability of the proteins' appearance, and no attempt is made to estimate the new proteins' properties."[3]

As stated in the previous chapter, mutations rarely result in positive improvements. In fact, most mutations are negative. Cancer is one example. Another example is

Delusion and Distortion

antennaepedia. This is where a fruit fly sprouts non-functional legs from its forehead instead of antennae. While this duplication of an existing complex structure does not seem to hurt the fly, no one would want an appendage growing out of one's forehead. Imagine if some humans grew non-functional thumbs out of their foreheads!

But what about the fruit flies? Would the leg-headed fruit fly be ostracized from the local feeding spot? Using the reasoning of natural selection, the need to feed might cause the flies to mutate functional forehead legs. That way they'd be better able to kick the other flies off of the feeding spot. Wow, the wonders of evolution!

In seriousness, the antennaepedia example is one that scientists have duplicated in a lab. They have also duplicated the alleged conditions of the primordial soup that gave rise to amino acids. Stanley Miller, a University of Chicago graduate student, duplicated the suspected conditions of the early primordial soup.

"Miller boiled the water and sparked the mixture of gases for about a week. During that time an oily, insoluble tar built up on the sides of the flask, and the pool of water became more and more reddish as material accumulated in it. At the end of the week Miller analyzed the mixture of chemicals dissolved in the water and saw that it contained several kinds of amino acids," explains Behe in *Darwin's Black Box*.

"Sustained effort by a number of workers eventually paid off; almost all of the twenty naturally occurring types of amino acids have been detected in the origin-of-life experiments."[4] Miller's work is impressive in that it shows the power legitimate sciences like chemistry.

But it also shows the undeniable complexity of life. Miller's successful synthesis of naturally-occurring amino acids took time to develop. He began with the goal of trying to replicate the alleged primordial soup that some believe gave rise to all life on earth. But to even get inside the lab to do these things, he invested years of study in the various disciplines related to his successful experiment. Yet evolutionary thought says that Miller's hard work could have just as easily resulted from random chance.

Could a blind, directionless process could have just as easily conjured up what Miller spent considerable time making? The obvious answer is that Miller's work did not result from random chance. Just like such a complex primordial soup, if it existed, could not have just popped up by accident.

While these things are impressive, a duplicate is a far cry from the original. For instance, the beautiful paintings can be easily and quickly duplicated with a camera, but if that original work did not exist, you'd have nothing to photograph. The duplications show the advancement and discipline that are required of real sciences, but they are still just duplicates.

One thing that some evolutionists have tried to duplicate is a missing link between humans and whatever hominid du jour tickles their imaginations. The hoax of Nebraska man is an excellent example of evolutionary ambition overriding scientific discipline. In 1922, Henry Fairfield Osborne found a tooth in Nebraska that became the foundation for the illustration of Nebraska man which appeared in *The Illustrated London News* on June 24, 1922.

"Some time after the initial discovery, an identical tooth was found by geologist Harold Cook," states Hanegraaff in *The Face That Demonstrates the Farce of*

Evolution. "This time the tooth was attached to an actual skull, and the skull was attached to the skeleton of a wild pig."[5]

Peking man is an even more outrageous hoax than Nebraska man. It also shows how greed plays a part in the agenda science of evolution. During a 1927 expedition in China, Dr. Davidson Black, a Canadian physician, conveniently discovered a tooth just as he was about to run out of grant money.

"The Rockefeller Foundation rewarded this discovery with a generous grant, permitting Black to continue digging."[6] Two years later, Black discovered the braincase of what appeared to be a primitive man. Based on nothing more than a tooth and a bashed-in skull, Black labeled it 'Peking man' and claimed it to be 500,000 years old. But in the years following Black's death, further research into Peking man proved that the skull was that of a monkey.

The undeniable fact is this: we have more fossils available now than in Darwin's day but we are not one bit closer to finding a missing link. The only things we have are pseudo scientists who are desperate to annihilate the

Delusion and Distortion

existence of God. There is a reason why the 'missing link' is still missing: it does not exist! Imagination and wishful thinking are the only place where you'll find a transitional form between different species.

Delusion and distortion are so essential to promoting evolution that pseudo scientists have to compare evolution to gravity, just to gain legitimacy. In a lame attempt at humor, a mock article that appeared at TheOnion.com called 'Intelligent Falling' attempted to pair the objections to evolution to phony objections to gravity.

The term 'intelligent falling' was supposed to satirize the Intelligent Design movement, which advocates a purpose for our existence. Again, this pathetic attempt at humor shows how fact-deficient the evolutionists are. To suggest that the provable scientific law of gravity is in any way equal to the bogus wannabe pseudoscience of evolution just shows how they are blinded by their own agendas.

The evidence of evolution's fraud status is abundantly clear, but I cannot close this chapter without mentioning the hoaxmaster-in-chief, German biologist Ernst Haeckel. Known for championing the bogus idea that 'Ontogeny Recapitulates Phylogeny' (ORP), Haeckel pressed evolutionary dogma in Germany the way that Huxley did in Great Britain. ORP, in plain English, means that an emerging human embryo goes through the supposed evolutionary stages where it is "a fish, a frog and finally a fetus." [7]

During the 'fish stage' of human embryonic development, according to ORP, a fetus has gill slits like those of a fish. This is based on the appearance of supposed gill slits that Haeckel observed in embryos. However, a developing human embryo does not, at any time, have gill slits. Haeckel used dishonest data and deceptive drawings to bamboozle the scientific community. It did not work.

"His dishonesty was so blatant that he was charged with fraud by five professors and convicted by a university court at Jena." [8] Haeckel's blatant forgeries were fully exposed in the 1911 book called *Haeckel's Frauds and Forgeries*. Even though Haeckel's phony assertions were easily dismantled in the early 20th century, the idea that ontogeny recapitulates phylogeny continues today. In 1977

Delusion and Distortion

Harvard professor Steven Jay Gould's book *Ontogeny and Phylogeny* resuscitated the proven hoax of ORP. Gould wrote that ORP was "one of the great themes of evolutionary biology."[9]

The rationalizations never cease to amaze me. They'd be laughable if they were not taken as serious science by so many people who should know better. This happens in spite of the fact that genetics proves that embryos do not change species during development.

"Although Haeckel's law has been discredited, another interpretation of the relationship between ontogeny and phylogeny survives under the name Von Baer's Law," writes Phillip E. Johnson in the book *Darwin on Trial*. "This hypothesis asserts that resemblances among embryos reflect levels of biological classification, so that all vertebrates, for example, look very similar in early development but become increasingly dissimilar as they approach their adult forms."[10]

Another underreported fact about evolution comes from *Of Moths and Men*. "...Austrian-born logical positivist philosopher Karl Raimund Popper (1902-1994), whose distinction between science and pseudo-science powerfully shaped the standard criteria of the scientific method[,]...cited the theory of evolution as the most dismal example of nonscience masquerading as science."[11] Sir Popper, who was knighted in 1964, published *The Logic of Scientific Discovery* in 1935.[12] He also served as a professor of logic and scientific method at the London School of Economics from 1949 until retirement.[13]

The desperate willingness to make fiction into fact is the foundation of evolution's short history. Physics and chemistry never had this problem. Newton did not have to fake his ideas and the same holds true for Watt, Volta, Faraday and numerous other legitimate scientists. However Haeckel's hoaxes take a much more serious tone in the next chapter called 'Racist Roots Bear Poisonous Fruits.'

Racist Roots Bear Poisonous Fruits
Chapter 4

"The only thing necessary for the triumph of evil is for good men to do nothing."

British writer and statesman
Edmund Burke (1729-1797)

Images of what evolutionists believe early man may have looked like show amazing similarities. Rarely is 'primitive man' portrayed as blond-haired, blue-eyed and pale-skinned. The images promoted are those of dark-skinned, kinky-haired people who resemble Africans and Australian Aborigines. This is no coincidence.

An example of this appears in the June 23, 2003 issue of *Time* magazine.[1] Although today's evolutionists avoid the ugly racist history of their much-cherished dogma, Darwinism is deeply rooted in the idea that dark-skinned people were closer to apes than whites.

Evolution's assignment of ape status to the politically-powerless, dark-skinned people of Africa and

Australia was easy. In 1859, these groups were considered closer to animals than the Anglo, Northern European whites who were pushing evolution. My acronym W.H.A.L.E., which stands for White Honkey Atheist Liberal Elite, accurately describes these folks. Unfortunately, there is nothing funny about the decades of social Darwinism and scientific racism that led up to one of the greatest acts of evil in all of human history.

One of the early disciples of Darwin was German geologist Friedrich Rolle, who believed that black Africans were physically and mentally closer to apes than white Europeans.[2] Rolle has the unique distinction of being the first one to write a full-length book in German on human evolution. "In his book he discussed at length the role of warfare as part of the human struggle for existence. He brushed aside any moral considerations, since the 'right of the stronger' is not subject to morality. Besides, he argued, war brings progress by favoring the fittest and ridding the world of the 'less fit.'"[3]

Weikart's book *From Darwin to Hitler: Evolutionary Ethics, Eugenics and Racism in Germany* provides an unprecedented view of the blatant racism of Darwin's early advocates. The book also uncovers the use of war by the Germans to help make evolution happen. "With only a few exceptions, most Darwinists, even the most ardent pacifists, considered non-European races inferior and condoned warfare if it resulted in the destruction of 'inferior races.' [War] would also provide scientific sanction for militarism in an age in which science was gaining prestige and for some intellectuals—becoming the sole arbiter of truth."[4]

"Evolutionary theory in general and Darwinism in particular had a tremendous impact on German thought," writes Weikart. "Already in the 1860s and 1870s, many young German biologists began promoting Darwinism. By the 1890s so many biologists and social theorists had tried to apply the Darwinian struggle for human existence to human society that Ludwig Woltman...began referring to them collectively as social Darwinists."[5]

Sydney J. Jones' book *Hitler in Vienna, 1907-1913* reinforces this point. "The intellectual atmosphere of Europe was alive with such race ideology by 1900, spawned by an oversimplification and extrapolation of Darwin's 'survival of the fittest' to the social scale."[6]

Social Darwinists believed that racial extermination was simply the byproduct of evolution. "Many Darwinian biologists and social theorists explained that racial extinction was inescapable and even beneficial, for it brought about evolutionary progress for the species as a whole," writes Weikart.[7]

It's important to remember that the subtitle of Darwin's book, *The Origin of Species*, is *The Preservation of Favoured Races in the Struggle for Life*. While today's apologists for evolution say that 'race' refers to animal groups, there is no denying the fact that evolution was the common thread in the decades of social Darwinism that led up to the Holocaust. "From the 'preservation of the favoured races in the struggle for life,' it was a short step to the preservation of favored individuals, classes, or nations," writes Gertrude Himmelfarb in *Darwin and the Darwinian Revolution*.[8]

"Social Darwinism has often been understood in this sense: a philosophy exalting competition, power, and violence over convention, ethics, and religion. Thus it has become a portmanteau of nationalism, militarism, and dictatorship, of the cults of the hero, the superman, and the master race. The hero or superman, most recently translated as Fuhrer, is assumed to be the epitome of the fittest, the best specimen of his breed, the natural ruler who exercises his rule by right of might."[9]

Social Darwinism quickly became part of the academic diet after Darwin's 1859 publication of *The Origin of Species*. Oscar Peschel, the editor of *Das Ausland*, a German scholarly journal on ethnology and geography, started promoting social Darwinism (aka racial extermination) just one year after the publication of *The Origin of Species*. Peschel believed that when the 'higher races' came into contact with the 'lower races', the lower races would stop reproducing and kill their own offspring. According to Peschel, these natives simply had no desire to keep on living once they came into contact with Caucasians.[10]

Blatant racism was commonly accepted, even among educated elites, in the pages of *Das Ausland*. In an 1860 journal article titled "Man and Ape," Peschel wrote the following piece of scientific bigotry: "The Negro is far removed from the European...Also the Negro is more animal, in that it gives off a disgusting odor, distorts its face in grimaces and its voice has a harsh, grating tone."[11]

By 1871, Peschel's work in the field of ethnology—scientific racism—was so highly regarded that the University of Leipzig offered him a professorship in geography. Four years later, professor Peschel wrote his most important book on scientific racism titled, appropriately enough, *Ethnology*.

Friedrich Hellwald, who succeeded Peschel as editor of *Das Ausland*, was also a Darwinian ethnologist who believed that 'inferior races' were doomed to extinction. Hellwald believed that Australian aborigines were the lowest race in the world and that the extermination of 'inferior races' was the natural result of progress.[12] This was 'survival of the fittest' applied to human beings.

Hellwald even chastised the British for ending slavery because he believed that it would result in the extinction of blacks. In his view, blacks could survive as slaves, but could "not compete with the white races in free competition."[13] Pushing the racist pseudo science of ethnology in *Das Ausland* was not enough for Hellwald. His 1875 book *The History of Culture* displayed overt anti-Semitism by labeling Jews as unable to produce "great statesmen or artists (except musicians)." He praised the English for their enterprising disposition, but labeled South Americans as lazy and African blacks as mentally inferior.[14]

Zoologist Karl Vogt, another prominent advocate of racial inequality, believed that the three races of humans descended from different species of apes. He believed that black Africans were closer to apes than Europeans and that non-Europeans were mentally inferior to Europeans. Vogt was no minor player in the scientific racism of his day. In 1870, he helped start the German Anthropological society. Vogt, like Huxley and Haeckel, took Darwinian thought to heart and ran with it. In 1863, just four years after *The Origin of Species* came out, Vogt published his major anthropological work titled *Lectures on Man*.[15]

At about the same time Oscar Schmidt, a professor of zoology at the University of Strassburg, wrote about racial extermination by Darwinian evolution. He wrote and lectured on the scientific validity of human inequality and the cruel struggle for existence. To Schmidt, some races were 'mentally inferior' and stated that natural selection "is a pure question of might," not right.[16]

"Schmidt thus used science to displace ethics and sympathy, transforming racial extermination from an atrocity into an inevitable—and by implication, beneficial—phenomenon," according to Weikart.[17]

Botanist Ernst Krause was another leading advocate of Darwinian evolution in Germany. As the editor of the Darwinian-devoted science journal *Kosmos*, Krause believed "that the 'inferior' races were dying out as a result of contact with more 'civilized' races." Krause also believed that the death of the "lower" races would "widen the gap between humans and apes."[18]

A major shift in thought occurred over the decades following the 1859 publication of *The Origin of Species*. By the end of the 19th century, there was a "proliferation of books and articles discussing racial struggle. For some thinkers race became the universal key to interpreting history, society and culture."[19]

Ernst Haeckel, the hoaxmaster-in-chief, was one of those authors. In his 1904 book *The Wonders of Life*, "Haeckel devoted an entire chapter to racial inequality entitled 'The Value of Life.' Therein he argued forthrightly that not all people's lives have the same value."[20]

Racist Roots Bear Poisonous Fruits

I'm not sure which is more stunning: the fact that one of the pioneers of evolution wrote such intolerant nonsense or that his bigotry is largely ignored by today's defenders of evolution. Unfortunately, today's intelligentsia is so in love with the false idea that science has replaced God that they are willing to sweep this genocidal racism under the rug, in the hopes that you'll ignore it. Thankfully, Weikart has exposed the ugly underside that evolutionists don't want you to see.

"According to Haeckel, 'the value of life of these lower wild peoples is equal to that of the anthropoid apes,'" writes Weikart. Haeckel's devaluing of 'primitive' races, by placing them on par with animals, would be the first step toward a genocidal mentality." [21]

Haeckel believed that "the most important aspect of Darwinism was the animal ancestry of humans, which would 'bring forth a complete revolution in the entire world view of humanity.'" [22] Unfortunately, Haeckel's prediction turned out to be true. The world view of evolution helped pave the way for the Holocaust and the acceptance of moral relativism and atheism. "The theory of human evolution would 'necessarily penetrate deeper than every other advance of the human mind' and would help integrate all branches of knowledge," writes Weikart.[23]

Weikart accurately summarizes the slippery slope of decades of Darwinian thought with the following statement: "The increasing secularization of European thought in the nineteenth century, in tandem with Darwinian ideas, opened the door for racial extermination by sweeping aside traditional (Christian) moral objections and by reducing humans to soulless organisms.[24] This secularization of Northern Europe and North America in the late 19th century and the early 20th helped pave the way for eugenics and the Holocaust. An example of this decline appeared in 1896 when social Darwinist Rudolf Cronau asserted that 'lower races' were mentally incapable of 'higher culture.'[25]

Dr. Henry Morris points out how deeply ingrained evolution was in Hitler's beliefs in his book *The Long War Against God*. "Hitler believed in struggle as a Darwinian principle of human life that forced every people to try and dominate all others; without struggle they would rot and perish."[26]

German anatomist Hermann Klaatsch was another

who advocated evolution's racial superiority. Like Hellwald, he believed that slavery was beneficial for slave-holding whites and the black slaves. Klaatsch "denied that blacks could be educated very much, so colonial powers should not expend too much effort in this regard. He rejected the notion that people of different races should have equal rights," writes Weikart. [27]

The underreported racism of evolution is nothing short of amazing. Quotes that would create a furor today were common place at the dawn of the 20th century. The following statement by author H.G. Wells is an excellent example: "There is only one sane and logical thing to be done with a really inferior race, and that is to exterminate it." [28]

No amount of absurd rationalizations, contortions of truth or revisionist history will allow evolutionists to weasel out of the undeniable fact their precious theory is racist. Simply assigning ape status to those who are not white and Northern Europeans does not work when you are trying to make your mark in the age of enlightenment. Sir Isaac Newton helped make the field of physics legitimate. Charles Boyle did the same thing with chemistry.

Darwin and his disciples have tried, unsuccessfully, to make evolution legitimate by masquerading within the real science of biology.

So, to manufacture scientific legitimacy for an illegitimate science, the term eugenics was created. The term, which comes from a Greek term for 'good in birth,' started as a way to see why some family bloodlines had so many successful people. Darwin's cousin, Sir Francis Galton, popularized the field of eugenics in the mid 1860s and it became the new school of thought among the Darwinists in the latter half of the 19th century. Galton's 1869 book *Hereditary Genius: an Inquiry into its Laws and Consequences* displayed the foundation of his eugenic views.[29]

In the book Galton "purported to show that talent, like simple genetic traits such as the Hapsburg Lip, does indeed run in families; he recounted, for example, how some families had produced generation after generation of judges. His analysis largely neglected to take into account the effect of the environment."[30] Eugenics may have initially looked like a modified form of genealogy, where questions were raised and answers speculated upon as to why some people were successful. But in light of its connection to evolution, eugenics was destined to be destructive.

Madison Grant, the president of the New York Zoological Society and author of 1916 book titled *The Passing of the Great Race*, helped merge eugenics and social Darwinism even more. "Mistaken regard for what are believed to be divine laws and a sentimental belief in the sanctity of human life tend to prevent both the elimination of defective infants and the sterilization of such adults as are themselves of no value to the community. The laws of nature require the obliteration of the unfit, and human life is only valuable when it is of use to the community or race."[31]

Amazingly, Grant's racist rhetoric words make Hitler appear tame. In *Mein Kampf*, Hitler wrote that "...definite racial purity must be established. It will thus gradually become possible to found border colonies whose inhabitants are exclusively bearers of the highest racial purity and hence the highest racial efficiency. This will make them a precious national treasure to the entire nation; their growth must fill every single national comrade with pride and confidence, for in them lies the germ for a final, great future development of our own people, nay humanity." [32] Of course Hitler didn't seek to simply promote 'good breeding,' he tried to exterminate groups of people. Six million people paid the ultimate price.

With the ever-increasing normalization of evolution among legitimate scientists and the general public, the 'science' of eugenics gained added acceptance in the early 20th century. An example of this is Theodor Fritsch's *Handbook on the Jewish Question.* Fritsch, a leading anti-Semitic thinker in post-WWI Germany, saw eugenics as essential to renewing the German nation.[33] By 1931, when the 30th edition of his *Handbook on the Jewish Question* came out, Adolf Hilter wrote the following verbiage to promote the book: "Already in my youth in Vienna I thoroughly studied *The Handbook on the Jewish Question.* I am convinced that this work contributed in a special way to prepare the soil for the National Socialist anti-Semitic movement." [34]

But Hitler alone was not able to pull off the Holocaust. The normalization of evolution and eugenics over the decades made the horrific doctrine acceptable to hundreds of thousands of ordinary Germans. As Weikart expertly points out, scientific racism became mainstream in the early 20th century Germany. "Many biologists and anthropologists at major universities, as we have seen, embraced ideas about racial inequality, racial struggle, eugenics, and euthanasia similar to Hitler's views. This helps make intelligible the willingness of 'ordinary Germans,' and even more so, leading physicians and scientists to actively aid and abet Nazi atrocities.'"[35]

You can see additional evidence of this normalization of social Darwinism in the late 19th century by the actions of people like Jörg Lanz von Liebenfels, Georg von Schonerer and Houston Stewart Chamberlain. Lanz, who was a prominent Viennese racist, advocated the extermination of lesser races by social Darwinism.[36] "Lanz's race-based morality could justify all manner or immoral deeds, as long as they were perpetuated against 'lower races,'" according to Weikart.[37] "He compared people of 'inferior' races to weeds needing to be pulled out, because they were a financial burden on the 'better' racial elements."[38]

As early as the 1880s, the leader of the Austrian

Pan-German party Georg von Schonerer advocated hatred of the Jews. Weikart writes that Schonerer believed that "Jews were using their immoral biological character to try to destroy the morally upright Germans. His biological determinism led him to conclude that the only solution to this ethical dilemma was to destroy the immoral Jews." [39]

Houston Stewart Chamberlain, an Englishman who lived in Germany from age 30 until his death, was another who believed that social Darwinism needed help in achieving its goals. Weikart describes him as one of the "most influential anti-Semitic writers of the early 20th century." [40] Labeled the 'spiritual founder' of Nazism, he and Schonerer have the rare distinction of being mentioned in Adolf Hitler's famous manifesto *Mein Kampf*. Chamberlain's writings were read by Hitler during his time in Landsburg prison in the 1920s, which is also when Hitler wrote *Mein Kampf*. The admiration was mutual. In 1923, Chamberlain stated that Hitler would be Germany's savior. [41]

The views of Darwin and his contemporaries provide overwhelming evidence that these ideas equal Eugenics: that some humans were a lower life form than others. Hitler did this to the Jews and evolution does it to those with dark skin. One of Darwin's contemporaries was British physician Thomas Huxley. Nicknamed 'Darwin's Bulldog' for his fierce devotion to evolution, Huxley made a remarkably racist statement when he said "No rational man, cognizant of the facts, believes that the average Negro is the equal... of the white man."[42]

But in case you think Huxley's comments were isolated, consider the slang terms in our own language. In the *Cassell Dictionary of Slang* by Jonathon Green, the term 'ape' is listed a derogatory term for a Black person. This dates back to the mid 19th century.[43] In the same dictionary, the term 'monkey' is listed as an insult, especially when used since mid 19th century by Whites of Blacks."[44] This was no coincidence. The mid 19th century is when evolution rose to fame.

In a 2000 column, CSTNet.com writer Dr. Don Boys pointed out that Edwin Conklin, a professor of biology at Princeton University and president of the American Association for the Advancement of Science, declared that blacks had not evolved as far as whites. "Every consideration should lead those who believe in the superiority of the white race to strive to preserve its purity and to establish and maintain the segregation of the races, for the longer this is maintained the greater the preponderance of the white race will be." [45] Hitler would be proud.

Darwin, toward the end of his life, provided a chilling prediction of the Holocaust when he wrote in *The Descent of Man* "...the civilized races of man will almost certainly exterminate, and replace, the savage races throughout the world." [46] Darwin and his disciples such as Huxley and Haeckel and other evolutionists, over the latter half of the 19th century, laid the foundation for one of the greatest evils the world has ever known. Along with Frederic Nietzsche, whose scorching hatred of faith, prompted him to declare that 'God is dead,' these early adopters of Darwinism helped open the door for the Holocaust. [47]

Once you've convinced enough people that 'God is dead' and that man is all that exists, morality quickly dies. According to the Nazi sympathizers who helped Hitler build a racist empire of evil, preserving the weak was not needed. According to Weikart "When the Nazis finally implemented their 'euthanasia' program by Hitler's decree in 1939 after World War II began, they recruited many physicians with [favorable] views on social Darwinism, eugenics, and racism similar" to prominent German scientists and physicians.[48]

Physicians, who take an oath to 'first, do no harm,' played a pivotal role in the synthetic evolution of Nazi genocide. Joseph Mengele, the infamous 'angel of death' at the Auschwitz death camp, was one of the many doctors who helped murder many thousands of Jews. "The tragic irony of Mengele and his like-minded colleagues is that while committing some of the worst atrocities in all of history, he hoped his experiments would help improve the human race."[49]

Those who ascribed to the Nazi ideal believed in a human version of natural selection. They made this ideal into reality by systematically exterminating six million Jews during WWII. "I don't claim that Darwin and his theory of evolution brought on the Holocaust," wrote Edward Simon, a Jewish biology professor at Purdue University, "but I cannot deny that the theory of evolution, and the atheism it engendered, led to the moral climate that made the Holocaust possible." An important argument that Hitler used to support his programs of racial genocide of the Jews and other groups was that they were genetically "inferior" and that their interbreeding with the superior Aryan race would adversely affect the Aryan gene pool, polluting it, and lowering the overall quality of the "pure race."[50]

In reference to Hitler, Sir Arthur Keith wrote in *Evolution and Ethics* that "The leader of Germany is an evolutionist, not only in theory, but, as millions know to their cost, in the rigor of its practice. For him, the 'national front' of Europe is also the 'evolutionary front;' he regards himself, and is regarded, as the incarnation of the will of Germany, the purpose of that will being to guide the evolutionary destiny of its people" and "Christianity makes no distinction of race or of color; it seeks to break down all racial barriers. In this respect the hand of Christianity is against that of Nature, for are not the races of mankind the evolutionary harvest which Nature has toiled through long ages to produce?"

It's quite clear that Hilter believed in and practiced a human survival of the fittest doctrine. "In Hitler's mind Darwinism provided the moral justification for infanticide, euthanasia, genocide, and other policies that had been (and thankfully still are) considered immoral by more conventional moral standards," writes Weikart. "Evolution provided the ultimate goals of his policy: the biological improvement of the human species."[51]

Hitler wanted the Aryan 'super race' to be pure and he used genocide to achieve it. This synthetic evolution started with mandatory sterilizations, the killing of those deemed 'unfit' and ended with mass exterminations of Jews. "Many biologists and anthropologists at major universities, as we have seen, embraced ideas about racial inequality, racial struggle, eugenics and euthanasia similar to Hitler's views. This helps make intelligible the willingness of 'ordinary Germans,' and even more so, leading physicians and scientists, to actively aid and abet Nazi atrocities."[52]

Ernst Rudin, who was named director of the Kaiser Wilhelm Institute for Psychiatry in Munich in 1932, is one of many who helped Hitler start off the Nazi drive for a master race. Weikart explains that Rudin co-authored the official commentary on the 1933 Nazi sterilization law. "This compulsory sterilization law resulted in the sterilization of over 350,000 people on the basis of the alleged hereditary 'defects,' which included not only congenital mental and physical illnesses, but also alcoholism." Hereditary Health Courts determined who should be sterilized. [53]

"Rudin was an enthusiastic supporter of Nazi policies, serving on official governmental committees related to eugenics. In a January 1943 article—a year-and-a-half after the beginning of the Holocaust—Rudin not only praised the Nazi sterilization law and the Nuremberg racial laws, but he also extolled the Nazi's 'combat against parasitic foreign-blooded races, like the Jews and Gypsies.'" [54]

Nazi propaganda films also helped to persuade the masses of Hitler's evolutionary madness. Titles like *Hereditary Illness* (1936), *All Life is Struggle* (1937) and *Victim of the Past* (1937) helped to normalize the genocidal evil of Nazism.[55] While showing a disabled and disfigured person, the films narrator chastises the viewer for defying evolution. "In the last few decades, mankind has sinned terribly against the law of natural selection. We haven't just maintained life unworthy of life, we have allowed it to multiply. The descendants of these sick people look like this!"[56]

The idea that certain groups are inferior is essential to evolution. 'Mongoloidism' and 'Mongoloid Idiocy' were the early names given to children with the chromosomal abnormality that we now call Down's Syndrome. Eventually named for Dr. John Langdon Down, the initial term came from the racist belief that Asians, as a race, were not as fully developed as Caucasians. Of course, the racism of evolution also stated that Africans and Australian Aborigines were less developed than Asians.

Support for this assertion appears in one of the documents used in the 1925 Scopes Monkey trial. The 1914 biology text book *Civic Biology* by Hunter states the five races of man as Negro, Malay, American Indian, Mongolian and "finally, the highest type of all, the Caucasians, represented by the civilized white inhabitants of Europe and America."[57]

Hanegraaff, points out that this racism against Asians was just another version of the recapitulation theory—that human embryos had to develop into fully-human Caucasians. "...Stephen Jay Gould, who notes that recapitulation served as a basis for Dr. Down in labeling Down Syndrome as 'Mongoloid Idiocy' because he thought it represented a 'throwback' to the 'Mongoloid stage' in human evolution."[58] Hanegraaff also points out the fact that Henry Fairfield Osborn, a leading paleontologist during the early 20th century advocated this horrific racism. "…the Negroid stock is even more ancient than the Caucasian and Mongolian…The standard of intelligence of the average adult Negro is similar to that of the eleven-year old youth of the species Homo sapiens."[59]

It's amazing that people are so willing to ignore the harsh lessons of history. Whether it's glossing over the hoaxes of the past by not mentioning them in biology books or failing the remember the events that paved the way for mass genocide, evolution is viewed, by the mainstream media and academics who should know better, as the genius of science over the stupidity of theistic faith. *Haeckel's Fraud's and Forgeries*, Piltdown man, Java man, Peking man and other Darwinian fairy tales are rarely seen outside of this book and the sources that I've cited. This is the danger of the willful ignorance of those who take evolution at face value because they want to be seen as intelligent by academic and media elites.

Weikart tackles this problem head on: "When he embraced eugenics, involuntary euthanasia for the handicapped and racial extermination, Hitler was drawing on ideas that were circulating widely among the educated elites. Klaus Fischer has rightly stated, 'Adolf Hitler's racial image of the world was not simply the product of his own delusion but the result of the findings of respectable science in Germany and other parts of the world, including the United States.' These ideas were not dominant in German society, but they were in reputable and mainstream in scholarly circles, especially among the medical and scientific elites."[60]

While evolution did not create the Holocaust, it did grease the rails of society's gradual decent into the hell of genocide. When people talk of evil in the 20th century, the name 'Hitler' invariable comes up. Although he was born 30 years after the publication of *The Origin of Species*, society's decline was already in motion. Decades of atheist intellectuals normalizing the idea that humans are nothing more than glorified gorillas—and that Africans,

Aborigines, Jews and Asians were far less valuable than the mythical Aryan uber-race—helped set the stage for the Holocaust.

Gradual change over time is a partial definition of evolution. In the case of society's decline into genocide, evolution has been a smashing success. Again, Hitler would be proud.

How Genetics Disproves Evolution
Chapter 5

"There are none so blind as those who will not see."

Unknown

    The more we know about genetics, the more proof we have that evolution is a fraud. An example is Ernst Haeckel's idea that 'ontogeny recapitulates phylogeny,' which collapses in light of DNA. As we discussed in earlier chapters, 'ORP' says that human embryos go through various animal stages prior to birth.

    For this idea to be true, human DNA from the parent would have to change species and then change back while in the womb. The Genome project and common sense clearly show that human embryos never change species. Furthermore, DNA carries the instructions that dictate traits from hair color to disease susceptibility. These precise instructions imply that they were created by design and not accidentally formed by random chance. While similarities do exist among living creatures, the similarities end when you take a closer look.

"The more specific a gene, the more information it contains. In general, the more specific any message, the more information it contains. The information in a gene is the same as the information in the protein that it encodes," according to Dr. Lee Spetner's book *Not by Chance.*[1]

It's important to briefly explain a few of the basic elements of genetics. Tara R. Robinson provides an excellent explanation in her book *Genetics for Dummies.* "Chromosomes are the paired structures that are made up of chromatin, which contains DNA and protein." Humans have 46 chromosomes, which equals 23 pairs of the commonly seen double-helix structure in the nucleus of each somatic cell.

Within each chromosome is deoxyribonucleic acid, also known as DNA, is "the chemical molecule that serves as genetic material." Robinson adds that a "strand of DNA is a long chain a polymer" of nucleotides. "Each nucleotide of DNA contains a nitrogenous base, a sugar with five

How Genetics Disproves Evolution

carbon molecules called deoxyribose, and a phosphate group. Genes lie along the chain DNA. They are made of sections of nucleotides. Some genes can have many nucleotides; others just a few. Humans have thousands of different genes, which reside on different chromosomes, but on the same chromosome in all people. For example, the gene for cystic fibrosis is always found in the same location on gene number 7 in all humans."[2]

When the DNA facts challenge the fiction of evolution, the evolutionists typically state that Chimpanzees have a genome sequence that is 98.8% identical to ours and, therefore, we must be related to chimps and evolution must be true. But how accurate is this assertion? A January 2003 article titled '98% Chimp' from clarifies this issue.

It turns out that this assertion, according to the website, is based upon a selective look at two small parts of one of the 46 human chromosomes. I'll spare you all the technical stuff but the ScienceAgainstEvolution.org author summarizes it beautifully: "If you look at less than $1/100th$ of the total genome, you can find areas that are 98.77% similar!"[3]

Yes, we humans do have DNA that is similar to others. Since DNA is made up of the four base chemicals of adenine, guanine, cytosine and thymine, you could argue that the DNA of chimps, gorillas, squid, cats and every other living thing is identical to humans. However, this would be an absurd overgeneralization.

The problem that evolutionists have is that they refuse to take a closer look and understand the precise and directional engineering that makes up genetic material. They only advance the supposed evidence that appears to back up their bogus theory. This is why evolutionists, unlike engineers and real scientists, will forever be stuck in a cartoon-like fairy tale where fish can walk and reptiles can grow feathers.

For some folks, no amount of logic and factual data will change their view. That's why I use the term 'evoligion' to describe them. Some choose to rationalize the genetic evidence against evolution as a way to support it. A July 2004 article titled 'The Elder Statesman of Evolution,' on the ScienceAgainstEvolution.org website, summed this psychosis nicely: "The problem evolutionists have is that the theory of evolution doesn't make sense." [4]

How Genetics Disproves Evolution

Something else that doesn't make sense is the evolutionists' irrational idea that random mutations increase genetic information. An example is the idea that a fish needed to walk on land so it grew legs. This would be an example of an organism increasing genetic information to better 'evolve' to its environment. This would be laughable if not for the fact that some people actually believe it.

Spetner shatters this concept. "I have indicated in this chapter that there is no evidence that genetic information can build up through a series of small steps of microevolution. Mutations needed for these small steps have never been observed. By far, most observed mutations have been harmful to the organism."[5]

Dr. Pierre-Paul Grasse, an evolutionist of the Sorbonne, reinforces this point. "No matter how numerous they may be, mutations do not produce any kind of evolution."[6] In a September 2005 article called 'Gene Duplication' on the ScienceAgainstEvolution.org website hammered the idea of evolution increasing specific information. "...Random repetition of words does not increase information. If you buy two copies of *USA Today*, you won't get any more information than if you just bought one. Furthermore, the redundant words tend to increase confusion, not knowledge." [7]

But evolutionists want to have it both ways. If genetic information increases, it's supposedly proof of evolution. If genetic information decreases—such as the loss of a supposed human tail—it is also proof of evolution. Both assertions are false and the more we look at genetics, the more it condemns evolution to realm of pseudo science.

An example that evolutionists use to push the idea that evolution adds information is drug resistance. Insects that develop a resistance to the insecticide DDT, are, in the view of evolutionists, proof that an organism can build up information by mutations to protect itself. However, mutations do not increase information. Insects develop a resistance to DDT because they lose information, according to Spetner. "It becomes resistant by losing its sensitivity to the DDT. This loss is the result of a mutation that changes the site on the nerve cell at which the DDT molecule binds, preventing the DDT from binding." [8]

Since evolutionists are willing to believe that random mutations can build up specific and directional information to create complex, living structures, let's take a look at one of those systems: the human brain.

This non-technical overview, from *Genetics for Dummies* by Robinson, illustrates how impossible it would be for random mutations to conjure up a control system like the human brain:

> The cerebellum is the largest part of the brain and is the part responsible for consciousness. [It's] divided into left and right halves, which are called cerebral hemispheres. Each cerebral hemisphere has four lobes named for the bones of the skull that cover them: frontal, parietal, temporal and occipital. Specific areas of the lobes are responsible for certain functions, such as concentration, understanding speech, recognizing objects, memory and so on.
>
> At the center of the brain are the thalamus and hypothalamus, which form the structure called the diencephalon. The hypothalamus generates many neurosecretions, which are carried to the pituitary gland at the base of the hypothalamus. The hypothalamus controls homeostasis by regulating hunger, thirst, sleep, body temperature, water balance, and blood pressure. The pituitary gland is called the master gland because, along with the hypothalamus, it helps to maintain the homeostasis by secreting many important hormones.

At the base of the brain are the cerebellum and the brain stem. The cerebellum coordinates muscle functions such as maintaining normal muscle tone and maintaining posture. The brain stem is formed by three structures: the midbrain, the pons and the medulla oblongata. The spinal cord is a continuation of the brain stem that runs down through the vertebrae of the spine.

Reflex arcs are connections between sensory neurons, the spinal cord, and motor neurons. They are good examples of how the nervous system protects you by making you get out of danger almost before you realize you are in danger.[9]

Touching a hot frying pan is an example. The nervous system alerts you, immediately, that further contact with that hot pan is a very bad idea by delivering a pain message to your brain. Yet evolutionists want you to believe that this highly-engineered system could have been constructed by random mutations. This is one of the many reasons why evolution is a fraud.

Another interesting genetic fact comes from the ScienceAgainstEvolution.org website. In an e-mail called 'DNA Evidence Failed' the author hammers the idea of organisms gradually becoming more and more complex."If evolution were true, one might expect the oldest, least developed forms of life to have the fewest chromosomes. It isn't too surprising that a worm has 2 chromosomes and a mosquito has 6. Man has 46 chromosomes, so he is almost as highly developed as a potato, which has 48. Maybe some day man will evolve into a goldfish (94) or even a shrimp (254)." Evolutionists want desperately to believe that genetics proves their cherished theory, but the facts are not on their side.[10]

Another genetic fact that is not on the side of evolutionists is Gregor Mendel's famous experiment with cross breeding. Mendel, an Austrian monk from the mid 19th century, is famous for cross breeding pea plants to see what would happen when different traits, such as color and height, were mixed when planted together.

Instead of getting a genetic compromise between tall and short pea plants, he discovered that some traits were dominant and some were recessive. The same principle applies to humans. An example is eye color. A normal mother with blue eyes and a normal father with brown eyes will have a normal brown-eyed child. This is because the brown trait is dominant and the blue trait is recessive.

Some evolutionists may try to use Mendel's work to justify evolution, but it simply shows how desperate they are to validate their false theory. Mendel showed how genetic factors interacted during breeding and their results. To suggest that Mendel's work somehow validates evolution in the slightest bit, simply shows how desperate and intellectually vacant evolution's supporters are.

But just when I think evolutionary reasoning has hit rock bottom, some evolutionists have begun to dig. Some view mutations as positive change that gives an organism an advantage over another. Aside from the undeniable fact that mutations almost always harm the organism, the question that must be raised is why one organism got an advantage and the other did not.

Did one need to survive more than the other? Why was one animal the predator and the other the prey? The evolutionary answer will always fall into one of the following categories: 1.) Fabricate a 'new theory' to account for this and get your ivory-tower comrades to buy off on it or 2.) Say that the questioner is a just not smart enough to understand evolution's complexity. Don't fall for either one.

How Genetics Disproves Evolution

Evolution has to masquerade behind the legitimate field of biology because many scientists simply default to this position. Matt Ridley, in his book *Genome: The Autobiography of a Species in 23 Chapters*, does this several times. After explaining the complex engineering of a chromosome, he simply defaults to evolution as the designer. So does James Watson in his book *DNA*. This is what I call Evolutionary Default Mode (EDM).

While Ridley and Watson do excellent work in explaining genetics, it's amazing that they just assume that evolution created these complex systems. Most scientists who are working in their respective disciplines don't have the time to research the validity of evolution and don't want to be demonized by their peers as being 'unscientific.' So, defaulting to evolution is easier.

But ignorance abounds among those who adamantly adhere to evolution. Genetics, basic scientific method and common sense are discounted in the devotion to the atheistic pseudoscience of evolution. In the next chapter, you'll see easy-to-understand evidence of why evolution is mathematically impossible.

Mathematically Impossible
Chapter 6

"The probability of life originating from accident is comparable to the probability of the unabridged dictionary resulting from an explosion in a printing shop."

> Princeton biology professor and evolutionist Dr. Edwin G. Conklin (1863-1952) quoted in *Darwin's Demise*

The idea that trillions of random variations and genetic mutations over billions of years magically turned ape-like creatures into astronauts is absurd. The odds are overwhelmingly against it, even though evolutionists cling to the idea that natural selection explains the rise of complex systems like the human eye and brain.

One of the ideas that mathematically-challenged evolutionists have promoted is the typing monkey theory. It states that if you have a million monkeys banging randomly on typewriters, they will eventually type the works of William Shakespeare. The alleged proof of this is a computer program written in the 1980s by Richard Hardison of Glendale College that, according to evolutionists, mimics what monkeys would do in an accelerated time frame.

In a June 18, 2002 ScientificAmerican.com article titled "15 Answers to Creationist Nonsense," author John Rennie wrote that the computer monkeys wrote the line "TOBEORNOTTOBE" within 90 seconds and recreated Hamlet in 4.5 days. However, Hardison's program had a huge advantage over a million feces-throwing simians stationed at typewriters—purpose. Hardison's experiment was designed and Hardison was the designer.[1]

In a reply to Rennie's article, the authors of ScienceAgainstEvolution.org countered that the specific 13-letter sequence was the only goal of the program. Another example of purpose. In addition to this, the typing monkey theory is a lame attempt by evolutionists to duplicate something that already exists. The monkeys typing a Shakespearean work or chemists making amino acids in a lab is nothing more than a duplication of a previously-created item.[2]

But what if scientists conducted a real-life experiment with actual monkeys and a typewriter? Well, the Arts Council of Great Britain coughed up over $3,700 (£2,000) to find out with an experiment performed by the University of Plymouth. According to a May 9, 2003 article from the BBC News website, "a single computer was placed in a monkey enclosure at Paignton Zoo to monitor the literary output of six primates. But after a month, the Sulawesi crested macaques had only succeeded in partially destroying the machine, using it as a lavatory, and mostly typing the letter 's'." [3]

According to Dr. Amy Plowman, the scientific officer for the Paignton Zoo, "the work was interesting but had little scientific value, except to show that the 'infinite monkey' theory is flawed." No kidding! But hope springs eternal among those who put on the experiment. "Director of the university's Institute of Digital Arts and Technology (i-DAT), Mike Phillips, denied that the project was a disaster and said they had learned 'an awful lot.'" [4]

The article stated that the money was for "hardware to set up a radio link so the activities in the enclosure could be watched live on a website (BBC). The six monkeys—Elmo, Gum, Heather, Holly, Mistletoe and Rowan—produced five pages of text which consisted mainly of the letter 's.' But toward the end of the experiment, their output slightly improved, with the letters A, J, L and M also appearing. However they failed to come up with anything that remotely resembled a word." [5]

So there we have it, folks. From a computer simulation designed to produce a specific 13-letter line of text to a group of university students watching monkeys defecate on a computer—proof that evolution's worst enemy is common sense.

Another mathematically-impossible pillar of evolution is the idea of spontaneous generation, which says that non-living things can create living organisms. Louis Pasteur's experiments in the 19th century disproved this absurd concept. He demonstrated the law of biogenesis, which states that life creates life. Nonetheless, some biology text books still treat spontaneous generation with reverence.

"What Pasteur showed was that life did not arise in his flasks under the conditions he used (sterilized nutrient medium, clean air) in the amount of time he waited. He did not show that life could never arise from nonliving matter

Mathematically Impossible

under any set of conditions."[6] Amazing! This biology textbook suggests that spontaneous generation would be possible if only Pasteur had not removed the bacteria from the flask—which was the whole point of the experiment!

Previous to this, most scientists believed that the decay of organic material was spontaneous. They did not realize that microscopic bacteria were getting into the material from the surrounding air. Pasteur showed that microscopic bacteria could be removed by sterilizing the environment. That's where the term 'Pasteurization' comes from. We 'Pasteurize' milk to remove harmful bacteria.

But who cares about facts when you are pushing an agenda and calling it a science? Along with discarding Pasteurization, evolutionists dismiss basic probability. In the book *Darwin's Demise: Why Evolution Can't Take the Heat*, authors Joe White and Nicholas Comninellis cite several examples of prominent scientists who show the mathematical impossibility of evolution. One is the late British Astronomer Sir Fred Hoyle, who calculated the probability of spontaneous generation at 10 to the 40,000th power. To illustrate the point, Hoyle stated in a 1981

Nature magazine article that "supposing the first cell originated by chance is like believing a tornado could sweep through a junkyard filled with airplane parts and form a Boeing 747." [7]

William Fix further illustrates this point in his book *The Bone Peddlers: Selling Evolution.* "Even if we take the simplest large protein molecule that can reproduce itself if immersed in a bath of nutrients, the odds against this developing by chance range from one in 10 to the 450th power (engineer Marcel Goulay in *Analytical Chemistry*) to one in 10 to the 600th power (Frank Salisbury in *American Biology Teacher*)...According to biologist Jean S. Morton, the odds against producing the 25,000 enzymes in the human body by chance are one in 10 to the $2,825,000^{th}$ power." [8] Fix also points out the fact that Francis Hitching, the author of the *Neck of the Giraffe*, stated that scientists generally rule out of consideration any event having less than one chance in 10 to the 50th power of occurring.

French mathematician Dr. Emile Borel, who's known for his work on the calculus of probabilities, affirms Hitching's point. "The occurrence of any event where the chances are beyond one in ten followed by 50 zeros is an

Mathematically Impossible

event which we can state with certainty will never happen, no matter how much time is allotted and no matter how many conceivable opportunities could exist for the even to take place." [9]

In spite of the overwhelming factual evidence against evolution, the mythology continues. A PBS documentary called *The Miracle of Life*, states that "Powerful winds gathered random molecules from the atmosphere. Some were deposited in the seas. Tides and currents swept molecules together. And somewhere in this ancient ocean the miracle of life began." [10] Amazing! This Emmy-award winning film says that it's all random chance. This is a prime example of an agenda—instead of the search for truth—driving science.

Another mathematical problem for evolution is the claim that because something changes, or mutates, in the case of genes, it increases information. Evolutionists claim that genetic copying errors can increase information, thus backing up natural selection. But, as Dr. Jonathan Sarfati explains in his book *Refuting Evolution 2*, "to claim that mere change proves that information-increasing change can occur is like saying that because a merchant can sell goods, he can sell them for a profit."[11]

White and Comninellis point out the absurdity of chance directing genetic improvements with a quote from Dr. I. L. Cohen. "To propose...that mutations [in] tandem with 'natural selection' are the root causes for 6,000,000 viable, enormously complex species is to mock logic...and the fundamentals of mathematical probability."[12]

The genetic information issue is not a new problem for evolutionists. In his 1984 book *The Bone Peddlers* Fix cited a 1958 book edited by S.A. Barnett called *A Century of Darwin*, where "British biologist C.H. Waddington writes '...a new gene mutation can cause an alteration only to a character which the organism had had in previous generations. It could not produce a lobster's claw on a cat; it could only alter the cat in some way, leaving it essentially a cat.'"[13]

Waddington is not the only one who dismisses evolution when it comes to genetics. Former Cambridge chemistry professor Michael Pitman reinforces the point: "Neither observation nor controlled experiment has shown natural selection manipulating mutations so as to produce a new gene, hormone, enzyme system or organ."[14] And this is after years of failed attempts by scientists to duplicate

Mathematically Impossible

natural selection in the laboratory.

In the previous chapter, we established that mutations, also known as copying errors, are almost always detrimental to the organism. Sir Ronald Fisher, an expert in the field of evolutionary mathematics, admits that "a single mutation, even if it is a positive one, has only a small chance of survival." [15] Add to this, the fact that even the late Carl Sagan, an evolutionist and atheist, stated that chance of life starting from non-living items is 1 in 10 to the two-billionth power. That's a lot of zeroes.

Another problem that faces evolutionists is the radiometric data that supposedly tells the ages of rock. Carbon 14 is one of the radiometric methods that geologists use. Theoretically, anything over 50,000 years old should have no detectable carbon 14 because the known rate of decay, or half-life.

But Dr. William F. Libby, who invented the carbon 14 dating method and won the Nobel Prize for chemistry, stated that the method is only accurate to about 4,000 years.[16] "Natural processes in general do not act at fixed rates," according to Dr. Kenneth L. Currie of the Canadian Geological Survey. "The assumption that an average rate taken over a long period of time can be extrapolated is generally unsatisfactory."[17]

White and Comninellis do an excellent job in showing the flaws in the radiometric methods. To make a concrete (pardon the pun) assessment of a rock formation's age, you have to know 1.) the quantity of radioactive elements that were in the rock when it formed, 2.) that the rate of decay is constant over time, and 3.) that no outside forces acted upon the rocks.[18]

So how can anyone say with any certainty how many radioactive elements were in the rock when it formed? They can't. They are making calculations based on false assumptions.

Basic geology tells you that there are three kinds of rocks: metamorphic, igneous and sedimentary. Each kind gets its name from the way it was created—by a physical force, volcanic activity or deposits by air or water. This established geologic categorization violates the third condition for getting an accurate rock age: that no outside forces acted upon the rocks.

But carbon 14 is not the only method. The potassium-argon (K-Ar) method is another. Argon, one of the most common radioactive elements, is a gas that can easily disperse out of rocks and can be added to rocks by meta-

Mathematically Impossible

morphic forces. But this supposedly perfect radiometric dating method is anything but accurate.

An example is a volcanic rock that came from Mt. St. Helens' 1986 eruption. When tested by the potassium-argon (K-Ar) radiometric dating method, it showed them to be 350,000 years old. In New Zealand, newly formed rocks from the Mt. Ngauruhoe volcano eruptions in 1949 and 1975 were radiometrically dated at 270,000 to 3.5 million years old. [19] *Darwin's Demise* sums up the rock dating issue nicely: "Determining the true age of rocks and fossils is inexact at best."

When faced with more and more mathematical and scientific evidence against evolution, Darwinian defenders claim that anti-evolutionists just do not know enough about natural selection. However, evolutionists have simply gone from their original theory of gradualism to Punctuated Equilibrium, popularized by evolutionist Stephen Jay Gould in the 1970s. Instead of gradual variations and mutations adding up to a species jump over millions of years, P.E. suggests that sudden, catastrophic changes made evolutionary species transitions.

So instead of gradual change over millions of years that's too slow to scientifically observe, we should believe that evolution happened in a bang that was too fast to see? Amazing! It must be nice to make up the rules as you go and get people to buy into the latest evolutionary fad.

Speaking of making things up, evolutionists would have us believe—contrary to the laws of physics—that a massive explosion called the 'Big Bang' started a process that made simple, lifeless particles into complex, organic systems. The idea is absurd, yet, like most of evolution, the promoters of this pseudo science have scammed this belief into the mainstream of our culture.

Anyone who has seen the photos of the devastation of Nagasaki and Hiroshima after the atomic bombings of 1945 has seen the disorder that explosions make. The houses and buildings were designed and built for specific purposes, but in a matter of seconds they were reduced to rubble. Yet, when it comes to the origin of life, we are supposed to suspend common sense and logic. Ironically, the evolutionists who despise any concept of God want us to take their words on faith.

Another area where evolutionists demand that we suspend our common sense is in the basic laws that Sir Isaac Newton established centuries ago. The second law of thermodynamics—which is just a fancy way of saying that

Mathematically Impossible

things left alone move toward chaos instead of order—is one the foundations of physics and can be easily displayed in everyday life.

An example of the second law of thermodynamics would be if you left your bicycle in the backyard for several months. After repeated exposure to rain that oxidizes (rusts) ferrous metals, sunlight that fades paint and heat that evaporates the moisture from rubber brake pads and adhesives, your bike would be, literally, falling apart. The chain would be rusted and susceptible to breaks, the tires would be flat and the shifting system might be too rusted over to work.

However, physicist and evolutionist James Trefil, who is also the author of *1001 Things Everyone Should Know About Science*, states that "...the Second Law holds only for isolated systems."[17] This is false! It holds true for countless systems that are not isolated, including the previously mentioned bike example. Physics, by definition, is the study of the physical world. Sir Isaac Newton, a Christian who founded modern physics and calculus, based the second law on real life examples that he tested in the physical world.

"Not only is the universe dying of heat loss, but

according to entropy—also known as the second law of thermodynamics—everything runs inexorably from order to disorder and from complexity to decay," writes Hanegraaff. "In evolution, atoms allegedly self-produce amino acids, amino acids auto-organize amoebas, amoebas turn into apes, and apes evolve into astronauts."[18] Physicist and mathematician Sir Arthur Eddington put it best. "If your theory is found to be against the second law of thermodynamics I can give you no hope." [19]

The precision of biological functions is another reason why evolution is mathematically impossible. For instance, the bombardier beetle ejects a poisonous fluid to defend itself. However, if these chemicals are not mixed precisely, the fluid will kill the beetle.

"Evolutionary theory has big problems when attempting to explain the existence and complexity of the bombardier beetle by means of random, chance happenings," according to Dr. Jobe Martin's book *The Evolution of a Creationist: A Layman's Guide to the Conflict Between the Bible and Evolutionary Theory*. "Each stage in the evolution of its special chemicals would have led to its destruction. This one-half inch insect mixes chemicals that violently react to produce something similar to an explosion. How could the bombardier beetle have evolved such a complex means of defense without killing itself in the process? This problem has the members of the evolutionary establishment scratching their heads. Evolutionary theory says that you lose it if you don't use it. But, how do you use it unless you have it in completed and in fully functional form?"[20]

Martin continues to explain how precise the engineering of the bombardier beetle has to be. "To prevent its own destruction, the little bug manufactures a chemical, called an inhibitor, and mixes it in with the reactive chemicals. But with the inhibitor, it would not be able to use the expulsion of hot, burning liquid and gases to discourage its enemies."[21]

In fact, evolution requires far more faith than the 'Bible-thumpers' that evolutionists so passionately hate. Evolution is an insult to real sciences like chemistry and physics. Biology, with its study of photosynthesis, cell function, anatomy and other legitimate topics, serves as the foundation of medicine and biochemistry. Similarly, physics serves as the foundation of civil and structural engineering by establishing physical laws of force and motion.

As any engineer or chemist will tell you, skyscrapers and disease-fighting drugs do not simply arise by chance. But evolutionists claim that natural selection is not random chance. They claim that the process of reproducing organisms—and the subsequent variations—generates complex systems like genetic code. But this is view is still based on random chance. Maybe they are advocating a new kind of math, called semi-random chance? This would not surprise me since evolution and semi-random chance are bogus concepts.

Another example is the complexity of the human eye. All of the things that have to work properly for the eye to function point away from the idea that random chance created this. Even the high priest of evolution, Charles Darwin, cast doubts about his own theory in *The Origin of Species*. "To suppose that the eye with all its inimitable contrivances for adjusting the focus to different distances, for admitting different amounts of light, and for the corrections of spherical and chromatic aberration, could have been formed by natural selection seems, I freely confess, absurd in the highest sense." [22]

But validity has yet to get in the way of evolutionary thought. Dr. Lee Spetner, a biophysicist and author of

Mathematically Impossible

Not by Chance: Shattering the Modern Theory of Evolution shows how astronomically remote the odds are that humanity is the result of chance. "When I compute the values of the chances (or probabilities) of some of the events of evolution, I'm going to get some very small numbers. They're so small that we don't have an intuitive feel for their size."[23]

When you look at the incredible complexity of DNA, it is folly to believe that humans evolved from some single-celled primordial ooze. Regardless of the amount of time, systems do not randomly go from simple to complex. This would require an increase in information. Spetner writes: "For cumulative selection to work, a lot of good mutations have to occur by chance. At each step of cumulative selection, a mutant with a positive selective value has to appear. It also has to be lucky enough to survive and eventually to take over the population. Then another good mutation has to appear for the next step, and so on. The neo-Darwinians seem to think the chance of all this happening is large enough to make evolution work. But no one has ever shown that to be so. No one has ever shown that such a thing is likely—or even possible!"[24]

It demands the existence of some kind of intelligent design. God, not random chance, dictated the intricate complexity of these organisms. Furthermore, to believe that God does not exist is just as absurd as believing in evolution. I call it the idiocy of atheism.

Why would random chance create an advanced society, after billions of years, out of some primordial ooze? The statistical odds of something as complex as DNA or the human eye forming by random chance are astronomically remote. But when you set up false premises and change the rules by whim, you can rationalize any kind of mathematical answer. Evolutionary math is easy—just add billions of years, lots of imagination and subtract your common sense.

Similarity Does Not Equal Ancestry
Chapter 7

"I believe that one day the Darwinian myth will be ranked as the greatest deceit in the history of science."

Dr. Soren Lovtrup quoted
in the book *Darwin's Demise*

Another cornerstone in the foundation of evolution is the idea that similarity equals ancestry. Monkeys, apes and gorillas—by evolutionary reasoning—must have a common ancestor with humans because there are common traits between these two species. The common ancestor is a step back from the original racism that stated that certain non-white, non-European races were closer to apes and gorillas than those white guys like Darwin, Huxley, Haeckel and Hitler.

Don't fall for the common ancestor line. It is nothing more than thinly-veiled racial bigotry. Roger Lewin points out the racism of evolution in his book *Bones of Contention: Controversies in the Search for Human Origins* when he cites a quote from a leading American zoologist named Louis Agassiz, who said "The brain of the Negro is that of the imperfect brain of a seven-month in the womb of a white."[1] To believe that apes and humans have a common ancestor, you'd have to believe that some groups of humans were, at one time, closer to the apes.

In an article titled 'Darwinism, Evolution and Racism' from the website Biblebelievers.net further exposes the racism of believing that humans and apes have a common ancestor. "As late as 1962, Harvard anthropologist Carleton Coon concluded that modern human races did not suddenly appear, 'fully formed as from the brow of Zeus', but that the differences between living races could be explained only in terms of their different evolutionary history, and that each major race followed its own evolution pathway.

Coon even writes that African civilizations were less advanced because black people were the last to evolve

Similarity Does Not Equal Ancestry

into modern humans. The first hominids may have arisen in Africa, he concluded, but the evolution of modern humans occurred in Europe and Asia."[2] As you recall, chapter four of this book addressed evolution's horrific foundation of racism.

Nonetheless, evolution is based on the concept all life evolved from a mass of single-celled, primordial ooze that magically made apes and astronauts from a common ancestor. But the argument that we came from a common ancestor loses its validity when images of an ape-like, slouching hominid is shown, in gradual phases, turning into an upright-walking human being. Evolutionists can shout 'common ancestor' all they want, but the history and popular images say something different.

From this point forward, I'll use the term ape as the catch-all for the non-relative that evolutionists assume is part of our family tree. Simian just doesn't have the same ring to it and I don't want to constantly shift from 'chimp' to 'monkey' to 'orangutan.' Now that we have that out of the way, I'll continue to prove why evolution is a fraud.

In *Bones of Contention* Lewin explains the

absurdity of evolution this way: "In the physical realm, any theory of human evolution must explain how it was that an apelike ancestor, equipped with powerful jaws and long, dagger-like canine teeth and able to run at a speed on four limbs, became transformed into a slow, bipedal animal whose natural means of defense were at best puny. Add to this the powers of intellect, speech, and morality, upon which we 'stand raised as upon a mountain top,' as Huxley put it, and one has the complete challenge to evolutionary theory."[3]

Of course, evolutionists themselves help to prove why evolution is a fraud. How? They counter with absurd theories that reject basic physics, chemistry and biology and smear those who disagree with them. You can always tell when anyone is losing an argument because instead of facts and logic, they use personal attacks. We'll get into this in greater detail in the next chapter, titled 'Agendascience.'

If we did come from some kind of ape-like common ancestor, it would be reasonable to assume that today's apes might share some basic functions with humans. For instance, humans have built upon previous knowledge. Our supposed ape relatives have not. These traits are

Similarity Does Not Equal Ancestry

indicative of humans because we see them in the civilizations that man has built, but they do not appear in apes. They still walk around the jungle, naked and throwing their feces at each other.

Humans, who have built upon prior knowledge by oral and written communication, have created and advanced societies over the years. The same cannot be said for apes. One of the most basic things that human beings do is create some kind of shelter or clothing. After that you have a progressive building of societies and civilizations. If we are so closely related to apes, as evolutionists suggest, why haven't apes done anything even remotely similar to this? Why have they not built shelters, made clothing, established societies and used technology to improve their lives, just as humans have?

While there are societal hierarchies among many animals it's a very basic 'leader-and-follower' structure that bears little resemblance to even the most remote human tribes. Another difference is in appearance. An overview of the photo book *The Secret Museum of Mankind* shows exemplifies the differences. One of the common threads that you see is that the people—even if they are in the ever-warm equatorial regions—are wearing clothes.

This fact goes against the assertion that evolutionists make that apes don't need to wear clothes because they live in warm climates. Another trend you'll see in the same book is that most of the humans are wearing some kind of ornamentation.

But evolutionists say 'look at the similarities.' OK, let's look at them. In the chapter 'Delusion and Distortion,' we established that Peking man and Nebraska man were famous frauds that were originally thought to be missing links. Let's look at another supposed 'missing link.'

The alleged missing link called 'Java man' (Pithecanthropus erectus) was supposed to be proof that apes were our relatives. Hanegraaff notes that "Java man consists of nothing more than a skull cap, a femur (thigh bone), three teeth and a great deal of imagination." Discovered in 1891 on the East Indian island of Java by Dutchman Eugene Dubois, he declared that he had found the 'missing link.' It's important to note that Dubois went to Indonesia to find the 'missing link' and came across his 'Java man' after four years of searching. [4]

Hanegraaff notes that even decades after Java man was proven to be a hoax, the media and prominent evolutionists consider Java man to be credible. "Despite all the evidence, it is truly amazing that *Time* magazine printed 'How Man Began,' an article that shamelessly treated Java man as though it were a true evolutionary ancestor. Even more incredible is the fact that David Johansson, best known for his discovery of a famous fossil named Lucy (after the Beatles' tune, 'Lucy in the Sky with Diamonds'), still regards Java man as a valid transitional form; and Harvard's Richard Lewontin thinks this information about Java man should be taught as one of five 'facts of evolution'."[5]

White and Comninellis perfectly summarize Dubois' find: "Dubois' announcement generated both attention and doubt. German zoologists tended to think Java man was actually an ape, the British considered it human and the French, something between the two. It was not until 30 years later that Dubois confessed to what else he had discovered at the same site" two skulls of modern humans. This immediately explained the human likeness of the femur. It also assured the scientific community that Java man was not a missing link at all, but actually a coverup! Ultimately, Dubois himself declared that the

Java man skull was simply a giant gibbon of the ape family."[6]

Neanderthal man is another supposed example of similarity equaling ancestry. "First discovered in a cave near Dusseldorf, Germany, Neanderthal Man is one of the most popularized 'prehuman' creatures. It is usually portrayed as a semi-erect figure, carrying a club..." write White and Comninellis in *Darwin's Demise*.[7]

However, as White and Comninellis state, "recent DNA evidence indicates that Neanderthal was fully human. Analysis made of the DNA within a Neanderthal skeleton was found to be markedly similar to that of modern humans, even when accounting for the fact that it was thousands of years old."[8]

White and Comninellis go on to write that "Many scientists agree that the various proposed 'ape-men' do not at all make up a series of evolutionary stages. Rather some were actually varieties of true humans, such as Neanderthals."[9] Add to this the fact prominent evolutionists doubt some long-held beliefs about Darwinian origins. One man who spent years trying to confirm the validity of evolution was Sir Solly Zuckerman. He came to the conclusion that "No scientist could logically dispute the proposition that man, without having been involved in any divine act of creation, evolved from some ape-like creature in a very short space of time (speaking in geological terms) without leaving any fossil traces of the steps of the transformation...The record is so astonishing that it is legitimate to ask whether much science is yet to be found in this field at all."[10]

Another evolutionary coffin nail comes from Dr. Robert Martin, senior research fellow at the Zoological Society of London, who said that "...popular books on human origins which were based more on fantasy and subjectivity than on fact and objectivity."[11] Evolutionist Lyell Watson also cast doubts on the common ancestor issue: "Modern apes, for instance, seem to have sprung out of nowhere. They have no yesterday, no fossil record. And the true origin of modern humans—of upright, naked tool-making, big brained beings—is, if we are to be honest with ourselves, an equally mysterious matter."[12]

But why let facts get in way when you have an agenda to push. Those plastered, ape-men models in natural history museums probably won't leave their exhibits anytime soon. The evolutionary crowd has too much invested in them.

As we discussed earlier, the pro-Darwinian crowd has gone to great lengths to keep evolution afloat, in spite of the overwhelming evidence against it. In the chapter 'Delusion and Distortion,' I explained the famous forgeries by Ernst Haeckel, who tried to hoodwink his peers with doctored photos. Sir Gavin de Beer of the British National History Museum, said that "seldom has an assertion like that of Haeckel's 'theory of recapitulation,' [been so] ...widely accepted without critical examination...." [13] Yet the falsehoods continue with another con job called Piltdown man.

'Piltdown man' is probably the biggest collision of wishful thinking and blatant deception in evolution's fraudulent history. Discovered in Piltdown Common in Southern England in 1912, Piltdown man consisted of fossils and bones crudely doctored to resemble a human's.[14] "The jaw seemed very ape-like and the skull resembled that of a human," write White and Comninellis of the fraud, which may have been the work of Arthur Smith Woodward, director of London's National History Museum and physician Charles Dawson.

Similarity Does Not Equal Ancestry

"They named the creature Eoanthropus dawsoni—or Piltdown man, and estimated him to be about 500,000 years old. Once again, their announcement generated enormous international attention and praise. However, by the 1950s a new technique was perfected to identify the age of bones. It was based upon measuring the concentration of fluoride that the bones had absorbed from the surrounding soil. Piltdown man's jaw was tested and found to contain no fluoride, proving that it was not a fossil at all and was only about a year old! The skull did contain fluoride, enough to date it at about 5,000 years old."[15]

There are other claims phony claims that evolutionists have made and will continue to make about how similarity equals ancestry. The point of this chapter is not to chase down every bogus theory that the advocates of this pseudoscience conjure up. The point is that the 'missing link' is still missing and will always be missing because evolution is scientifically invalid. But evolutionists continue to pass off evolution as if it is scientific fact. In the next chapter, you'll understand why evolutionists won't let go of their phony fairy tale.

Agendascience
Chapter 8

> "Materialists, atheists, and radical secularists had long displayed a certain fondness for evolutionary theories of origins…anything to dispense with God."
>
> Edward J. Larson from the book
> *Evolution: The Remarkable History of a Scientific Theory*

By now you know that evolution is not a science, but a humanistic philosophy that is based on hatred for God and an ignorance of legitimate science. Anyone with a basic understanding of physics, chemistry and mathematics can easily puncture the flimsy façade of evolution. Unfortunately, evolutionists' attempt to replace God with man as the ultimate authority has helped speed up society's decline into moral relativism.

"God became more than superfluous under Darwin's emerging view of origins—He became problematic," writes Larson in his book *Evolution: The Remarkable History of a Scientific Theory*. "At the very least, the theory of evolution dispenses with the immediate need for a Creator to shape individual species, including humans."[1] Hoaxmaster-in-chief Ernst Haeckel has credited Darwin for helping science to dismiss theistic faith. German physician Ludwig Buchner was another scientific materialist who popularized Darwinian evolution in the latter half of the 19th century. "Alfred Grotjahn, professor of social hygiene at the University of Berlin and leading figure in the eugenics movement, fondly recalled the time in his youth when he read Buchner's book, *Force and Matter*, which stripped him of all traces of religious faith," writes Weikart. "For them, [Darwinism] was a central ingredient of a new worldview that was locked in combat with traditional Christian religion."[2]

The acceptance of evolution is a symptom of a declining culture. How far can we drop when those who educate our children believe that God is a myth and that our ancestors were ape-like creatures? What happens to a society that believes that certain races are closer to animals than others? We can look back at history and say that we'll never repeat the horrors of the holocaust, but those words ring hollow when we repeat the same actions that paved the way for such an evil to take place.

The politically powerless and those deemed as 'lower races' were evolution's stepping stones. As mentioned in chapter four, racism is an inescapable fact of evolution. In the book *Darwin and the Darwinian Revolution*, Gertrude Himmelfarb writes that "Darwin himself, in spite of his aversion to slavery, was not averse to the idea that some races were more fit than others." [3]

Another reference to the racism of evolution rears its ugly head in Edward J. Larson's book *Evolution: The Remarkable History of a Scientific Theory*. Larson writes of Darwin's encounter with the native people of the southernmost tip of South America at Tierra del Fuego. Darwin viewed these people as the "...lowest form of humanity on earth." [4]

This racism also extended to Australia, according to Dr. Ken Ham's book *The Lie: Evolution*. "Many of the early settlers of Australia considered the Australian Aborigines to be less intelligent than the 'white man,' because aborigines had not evolved as far as whites on the evolutionary scale. In fact, the Hobart Museum in Tasmania (Australia) in 1984 listed this as one of the reasons why early white settlers killed as many aborigines as they could."[5] In addition, Ham cited a February 10, 1924, *New York Tribune* article that stated that 'the missing link had been found in Australia' and that it was the aborigines of Tasmania.

As you already know, evolutionary ideology helped pave the way for the Holocaust. It took decades of normalization of evolution for thousands of people to accept Hitler's ideology of racial purification, which the Nazis carried out by forced sterilizations and euthanizing those who were deemed to be a burden. The gas chambers soon followed.

In the book *Forced Exit: The Slippery Slope From Assisted Suicide to Legalized Murder*, author Wesley J. Smith explains that "this unethical approach to the practice of medicine [euthanasia] was already well developed in Germany by the time Hitler came to power in 1933. Indeed, euthanasia had been aggressively promoted as a proper and ethical public policy by the German medical, legal and academic intelligentsia since the late nineteenth century, when Hitler was a child." [6] Prior to 1859, there was little discussion of euthanasia, abortion or exterminating those deemed unfit. After the publication of *The Origin of Species*, these topics became mainstream issues.

So am I advocating the banning of evolution? No. When the Tennessee legislature passed the famous 1925 law that made the teaching of evolution illegal, it set up one of the biggest public relations events in the pseudoscience's short history. This hotly-covered news story became the basis for the movie *Inherit the Wind* and the countless stereotypical impressions that evolutionists carry forward to this day. One of the most important cultural impressions that came out of the trial, which Scopes lost, was that evolution is proven science; it is not. Another is the idea that those who disagree with evolution are bible-thumping hayseeds who are scientifically illiterate; we are not.

We don't need to ban evolution any more than we need to ban the flat-earth theory from geography classes. Evolution is a failure. The earth is not flat and the moon is not made out of green cheese.

I wrote this book because I was tired of the evolution debate constantly turning into a 'science versus religion' stalemate. I wanted to know how well, or poorly, evolution stood on its own. By now, you know that evolution is a fraud. But don't expect those who've spent decades working in 'evolutionary' fields to simply change their minds, even though the facts are solid and irrefutable. When evolutionists cannot argue ideas, they turn to personal attacks.

"If evolutionary biology is to be a science rather than a branch of philosophy, its theorists have to be willing to ask the scientific question: How can Darwin's hypothesis of descent with modification be confirmed or falsified," writes Philip Johnson in the book Darwin on Trial.[7] Another way to gauge the validity of evolution is to see how its treated by its peers. *The DK Ultimate Visual Dictionary of Science* is a great example. This 448-page reference book concisely and clearly explains each discipline—chemistry, physics, biology, geology, anatomy—of science. Yet it only devotes two pages to the section on evolution.[8] I'd say the editors were being generous, but the disrespect is obvious. In addition to this, the concept of Intelligent Design has gained momentum over the years because of the weakness of evolution.

At issue is how strong the theory of evolution is—not how weak or strong any other theory is. Again, the deflection to some kind of creationist versus evolutionist battle always appears when the facts do not support evolution. This book is not about advocating any idea on how life began.

But the evolutionary elite believe that they have all the answers, especially since 'they're too smart to believe in God.' Behe addressed this issue directly in *Darwin's Black Box*: "Stephen Jay Gould of Harvard University has made much of the panda's 'thumb.' The giant panda lives on a diet of bamboo. To strip the leaves off bamboo shoots the panda grips them in its paw with a bony protuberance that emanates from its wrist; the normal five digits are also present. Gould argues that a designer would have given the panda a real opposable thumb, and so he concludes that the panda's thumb evolved. He assumes the designer would act as he would, that pandas' thumbs 'ought' to be arranged a different way.

"He then takes those assertions to be positive evidence for evolution. Gould has never done the science to support his idea: he has not shown or calculated what the minimum extension of the wrist bone would have to be to help the panda; he has not justified the behavioral changes that would be necessary to take advantage of the change in bone structure; and he has not mentioned how pandas ate before acquiring the thumb. He has not done anything except to spin a tale." [9]

The key to defeating this modern-day flat earth theory is to stay on the facts. Evolutionists always want to attack those who question their sacred idea because they do not have the facts on their side. This pseudoscientific, agenda-driven form of racism is easily defeated with the information that you've just read.

What is amazing is the gall of those who think that once they know how something works, they can accurately state why that system was created. While Darwin did succeed in showing adaptation, he and his countless disciples over the past 150 years, have yet to show a valid species transition.

Hanegraaff sums this up nicely. "Colin Patterson,

senior paleontologist at the prestigious British Museum of Natural History, which houses the world's largest fossil collection-sixty million specimens-confessed 'If I know of any [evolutionary transitions], fossil or living, I would have certainly included them [in my book Evolution].' His statement underscores the fact that the fossil record is an embarrassment to evolutionists. No verifiable transitions from one species to another have as yet been found." [10]

"The Darwinian theory of descent has not a single fact to confirm it in the realm of nature," according to zoology & comparative anatomy professor Albert Fleishman. "It is not the result of scientific research but purely the product of imagination." [11]

It probably did not take many apples crashing upon Sir Isaac Newton's cranium before the explanation of gravity became clear to him. However, the same cannot be said of evolutionists. They've been sitting under the evolutionary family tree for decades while phony fossils and fraudulent finds pile upon their collective heads. Yet evolutionists continue to believe that their atheistic pseudoscience deserves a place in the real science of biology. They continue to discard basic probability, common sense and legitimate science to push their agendascience upon a like-minded media. Newton had the wisdom to get out from under that fabled tree and make scientific history. Evolutionists must have a splitting headache by now.

Another aspect of agendascience is that evolution was mandated by the communist government of the former Soviet Union. Dr. Henry Morris wrote in his book *The Long War Against God* that "...evolution through inheritance of acquired characteristics was promoted by not only Marx and Engels, but also by Lenin and Stalin. All of these men wrote extensively on biology, and two generations of Russian biologists were essentially forced to follow this official Communist Party position."[12]

Morris points out the interesting parallel between the theory of Punctuated Equilibrium and the official doctrine of the Communist biologists in the USSR. "When it finally became evident that controlled environmental evolution [gradual evolution] would not work, Communist evolutionists began to promote the idea of saltational evolution—that is, evolution in big spurts, brought about presumably by chaotic and uncontrolled changes in environment.

Agendascience

"It is significant that large numbers of university professors in this country today are Marxist in philosophy, though not many are actually members of the Communist Party. One of the most important is Stephen Jay Gould, who teaches biology, paleontology, and geology at Harvard University, and who is almost certainly the most articulate and influential evolutionist in America today. He and Niles Eldridge of the American Museum of Natural History have popularized the idea of 'punctuated equilibrium.'"[13]

Further proof of the agenda mixing with science comes from historians and biographers, such as Barzun. "Marx and Engels accepted evolution almost immediately after Darwin published *The Origin of Species*. Within a month, Engels wrote to Marx (Dec. 12 1859): 'Darwin, whom I am now reading, is splendid.' Evolution, of course, was just what the founders of communism needed to explain how mankind could have come into being without the intervention of any supernatural force, and consequently it could be used to bolster the foundations of their materialistic philosophy." [14] In *Darwin, Marx, Wagner: Critique of a Heritage* author Jacques Barzun writes that

"It is commonplace that Marx felt his own work to be the exact parallel of Darwin's. He even wished to dedicate a portion of *Das Kapital* to the author of *The Origin of Species.*"[15]

But the path did not end there. Morris explains that the acceptance of evolution helped the Soviets set up the official state religion of 'Scientific Atheism.' Again, evolution and atheism go hand in hand. In addition to this, evolutionists often cite the fact that Charles Darwin was a theology student, who left his Biblical studies to study biology. This fits perfectly into the atheist/evolutionist view that the pinnacle of intelligence is the acceptance of evolution and the denial of God.

Thomas Huxley, according to Adrian Desmond's book *Huxley: From Devil's Disciple to Evolution's High Priest*, wrote: "Man's challenger was no longer God, but Darwin's Godlike nature, which scrutinized every gambit, every move. Only the scientist was investigating nature's rulebook; only he could be society's new schoolteacher."[16]

Evolution is a faith. Harvard biology professor Dr. George Wald, who also won the 1971 Nobel Prize in biology, gives a shining example of this: "…I do not want to believe in God. Therefore I choose to believe in that which I know is scientifically impossible, spontaneous generation leading to evolution."[17]

It's utter nonsense to believe that humans evolved over billions of years from some single-celled primordial ooze. Regardless of the earth's age, systems do not randomly go from simple to more complex. It demands the existence of some kind of intelligent design. God, not random chance, dictated the intricate complexity of these organisms. Furthermore, to believe that God does not exist is just as absurd as believing in evolution. This is what I call the idiocy of atheism.

Another example of the precise engineering that goes against the idea of evolution is the Angler fish. This deep-sea dweller lives near the bottom of the ocean and uses a lighted, artificial worm that extends from its head, to lure its prey into striking distance. As Dr. Martin explains "this light displays highly advanced technology...a compound called Luciferin is oxidized with the help of an enzyme that scientists named Luciferase, and this reaction produces heatless light."[18]

Martin explains that "research scientists have broken down Luciferase into more than 1000 proteins, but they still do not know how the heatless light is produced."[19] Now, if we take the famous walking fish symbol that evolutionists so proudly display and apply it to the Angler fish, it raises countless problems for evolution.

How would a fish evolve from walking on land, to living in shallow water and then, eventually, take up residence under the bone-crushing ocean depth of 2000 pounds per square inch? All of this with a lighted lure extending from its head, used specifically to catch food.[20] This would be a comical fairy tale if not for the fact that otherwise intelligent people believe this to be scientific fact.

The facts are clear and the sources can be checked out. From the rejection of basic chemistry, physics and mathematics to the undeniable racism and genocide that evolution endorses, you now know why evolution is a fraud.

"Evolutionists have always struggled with the problem of how to promote their theory in the public arena. They believe evolution is a fact, yet according to polls many people are not so taken with the idea," according to

Darwin's God: Evolution and the Problem of Evil by Cornelius Hunter.

Ideas are powerful and they should be forced to stand in light of objective truth. Otherwise, up becomes down and right becomes wrong.

Weikart sums it up nicely: "Darwinism by itself did not produce the Holocaust, but without Darwinism, especially in its social Darwinist and eugenics permutations, neither Hitler nor his Nazi followers would have had the necessary scientific underpinnings to convince themselves and their collaborators that one of the world's greatest atrocities was really morally praiseworthy. Darwinism—or at least some naturalistic interpretations of Darwinism—succeeded in turning morality on its head."[21]

By this point, you can conclude that there are two reasons for believing in evolution: ignorance and defiance. Those who advocate evolution, in many cases, have a raging hatred for God. They don't want to be told that there is something called objective truth. They don't want to feel guilty that they are living outside the bounds of a moral society. So to alleviate this guilt, they deify themselves (university professors and elites) and claim that man is the ultimate authority. God is just opium for the masses, as a famous communist once said, and only dim-witted, uneducated huckleberries still rely on the mythology of faith.

This strategy has been successful because no one wants to be thought of as stupid. But who's the dummy when one group poses an unsupportable theory that is scientifically-invalid? Who's the idiot when your theory violates the fundamental laws of chemistry, physics and mathematics? This is the situation that our new secular society is in.

Evolution, at best, is a philosophical theory that does not belong in any science class. But, over the past decades, those with an atheistic agenda have ridden their walking fish into mainstream of our society without much of a fight. Those who raised doubts about evolution were demonized as backward hayseeds, stuck in the dark ages, who were fighting against the facts of science.

What's most annoying is that our society has just rolled over and allowed this to happen. This was the complacency in the latter half of the 19th century that allowed the elevation of man over God to take root.

Decades passed and the results were horrific. Remember the famous quote from Edmund Burke: "All that is necessary for evil to triumph is that good men do nothing."

ACKNOWLEDGEMENTS

I must thank Hank Hanegraaff, Richard Weikart, Joe White, Nicholas Comninellis, Ken Ham and Jonathan Sarfati for their books, which served as research sources for *Why Evolution is a Fraud: A Secular and Common-Sense Deconstruction*. I also thank the folks at www.ScienceAgainstEvolution.org for their invaluable work. Most of all, I thank God for His infinite blessings.

ABOUT
THE
AUTHOR

Tom Sutcliff is a former copywriter, editor and technical writer who lives in the United States.

NOTES

Chapter 1–Why It Matters

    1. Maiklem, pp. 20-21

    2. Barzun, p. 70

    3. Weikart, p. 216

    4. Magee, p. 172

    5. Morris, p 72

    6. Weikart, p. 229

    7. Ibid, p. 230

Chapter 2–Adaptation, Not Evolution

    1. Hanegraaff, p. 33

    2. Comninellis & White, p. 119

    3. www.ScienceAgainstEvolution.org

    4. Hooper, inside flap

    5. Ibid, prologue p. xviii

    6. Maiklem, p. 263

    7. Hanegraaff, p. 37

    8. Ibid, p. 36

    9. Ibid, p. 36

    10. Comninellis & White, p. 85

    11. Hanegraaff, p. 33

    12. Trefil, p. 55

Chapter 3–Delusion and Distortion
>   1. Behe, p. 78
>   2. Ibid, p. 78-79
>   3. Ibid, p. 91
>   4. Ibid, p. 167
>   5. Hanegraaff, p. 49
>   6. Ibid, p. 54
>   7. Ibid, p. 95
>   8. Ibid, p. 94
>   9. Ibid, p. 94
>   10. Johnson, p. 72
>   11. Hooper, p. 213
>   12. Encyclopedia.com
>   13. Williams, p. 273

Notes

Chapter 4–Racist Roots Bear Poisonous Fruits

1. Time, pp. 56-58
2. Weikart, p. 189
3. Ibid, p. 167
4. Ibid, p. 165
5. Ibid, pp. 10-11
6. Jones, p. 118
7. Weikart, p. 8
8. Himmelfarb, p. 416
9. Ibid, p. 416
10. Weikart, p. 188
11. Ibid, p. 112
12. Ibid, pp. 188-189
13. Ibid, p. 189
14. Ibid, p. 112
15. Ibid, p. 110
16. Ibid, p. 190
17. Ibid, p. 191
18. Ibid, pp. 191-192
19. Ibid, p. 195
20. Ibid, p. 108
21. Ibid, pp. 109-110
22. Ibid, p. 11

Chapter 4–Racist Roots Bear Poisonous Fruits (continued)

23. Ibid, p. 11
24. Ibid, p. 185
25. Ibid, p. 183
26. Morris, p. 79
27. Weikart, p. 116
28. Ibid, p. 185
29. Watson, p. 18-19
30. Ibid, p. 18-19
31. Weikart, p. 10
32. Hitler, p. 405
33. Weikart, p. 224
34. Ibid, p. 224
35. Ibid, p. 225
36. Ibid, p. 199
37. Ibid, p. 218
38. Ibid, p. 218
39. Ibid, p. 220
40. Ibid, p. 220
41. Ibid, p. 220

Notes

Chapter 4–Racist Roots Bear Poisonous Fruits (continued)

    42. Boys, CSTnet.com, Evolution: Basis for Racism

    43. Green p. 24

    44. Ibid, p. 799

    45. Boys, CSTnet.com, Evolution: Basis for Racism

    46. Comninellis & White, p. 154

    47. Magee, p. 172

    48. Weikart, p. 226

    49. Ibid, p. 227

    50. Morris, p. 78

    51. Weikart, p. 215

    52. Ibid, p. 225

    53. Ibid, p. 225

    54. Ibid, p. 226

    55. Ibid, p. 226

    56. Ibid, p. 226

    57. www.law.umkc.edu/faculty/projects/ftrials/scopes

    58. Hanegraaff, p. 100

    59. Ibid, pp. 101-102

    60. Weikart, p. 232

Chapter 5–How Genetics Disproves Evolution
1. Spetner, p. 134
2. Robinson, p. 244
3. www.ScienceAgainstEvolution.org
4. Ibid
5. Spetner, p. 159
6. Comninellis & White, p. 43
7. www.ScienceAgainstEvolution.org
8. Spetner, p. 143
9. Robinson, p. 187
10. www.ScienceAgainstEvolution.org

Chapter 6–Mathematically Impossible
1. www.ScientificAmerican.com, June 18, 2002
2. www.ScienceAgainstEvolution.org
3. www.BBCnews.com, No Words to Describe Monkeys' Play
4. Ibid
5. Ibid
6. Arms & Camp, p. 292
7. Comninellis & White, p. 34

Notes

Chapter 6–Mathematically Impossible (continued)

   8. Fix, pp. 196-197
   9. Ibid
  10. Hanegraaff, p. 70
  11. Sarfati, p. 56
  12. Comninellis & White, p. 43
  13. Fix, pp. 197
  14. Comninellis & White, p. 47
  15. Spetner, p. 54
  16. Comninellis & White, p. 63
  17. Ibid, p. 64
  18. Ibid, p. 64
  19. Ibid, p. 65
  20. Hanegraaff, p. 85
  21. Ibid, p. 85-86
  22. Martin, p. 40
  23. Ibid, p. 41
  24. Comninellis & White, p. 44
  25. Spetner, p. 93
  26. Ibid, p. 91

Chapter 7–Similarity Does Not Equal Ancestry

1. Lewin, p. 306
2. www.BibleBelievers.net
3. Ibid
4. Hanegraaff, p. 50
5. Ibid, p. 52
6. Ibid, p. 112
7. Comninellis & White, p. 114
8. Ibid, p. 114
9. Ibid
10. Ibid, p. 118
11. Ibid
12. Ibid
13. Hanegraaff, p. 94
14. Ibid, pp. 52-54
15. Comninellis & White, pp. 115-116

Notes

Chapter 8–Agendascience

1. Larson, p. 69
2. Weikart, p. 12
3. Himmelfarb, p. 416
4. Larson, p. 67
5. Ham, p. 102
6. Smith, p. 72
7. Johnson, p. 71
8. Maiklem, p. 20
9. Behe, pp. 228-229
10. Hanegraaff, p. 33
11. Comninellis & White, p. 126
12. Morris, p. 87
13. Ibid, p. 87
14. Ibid, p. 83
15. Barzun, p. 8
16. Desmond, p. 363
17. Comninellis & White, p. 47
18. Martin, p. 159
19. Ibid, pp. 159-160
20. Martin, pp. 159-160
21. Hunter, p. 90
22. Weikart, p. 233

BIBLIOGRAPHY

Arms, Karen & Camp, Pamela S.
> *Biology*
> Saunders College Publishing, 1982, 2nd Edition
> Philadelphia, Pennsylvania

Barzun, Jacques
> *Darwin. Marx Wagner: Critique of a Heritage*
> Doubleday, 1981, Reprint of Revised 2nd Edition
> (Phoenix Edition)
> Garden City, New York

Behe, Michael
> *Darwin's Black Box: The Biochemical Challenge to Evolution*
> Free Press (Simon & Schuster), 1996
> New York, New York

Boys, Don
> 'Evolution: Basis for Racism!'
> www.CSTNet.com, 2000

Caspari, Rachel & Wolpoff, Milford H.
>   *Race and Human Evolution*
>   Simon and Schuster, 1997
>   New York, New York

Comninellis, Nicholas & White, Joe
>   *Darwin's Demise: Why Evolution Can't Take the Heat*
>   Master Books, 2001
>   Green Forest, Arkansas

Desmond, Adrian J.
>   *Huxley: From Devil's Disciple to Evolution's High Priest*
>   Michael Joseph Ltd, 1997
>   United Kingdom

Fix, William
>   *The Bone Peddlers: Selling Evolution*
>   MacMillan/Scribner, 1984
>   New York, New York

Bibliography

Green, Jonathan
>	*The Cassell Dictionary of Slang*
>	Cassell, 1999, 2nd,
>	United Kingdom

Ham, Ken
>	*The Lie: Evolution*
>	Master Books, 1987
>	Green Forest, Arkansas

Hamann, Brigitte
>	*Hitler's Vienna: A Dictator's Apprenticeship*
>	Oxford University Press, 1999
>	New York, New York

Hanegraaff, Hank
>	*The Face That Demonstrates the Farce of Evolution*
>	W Publishing Group, 1998
>	Nashville, Tennessee

Himmelfarb, Gertrude
> *Darwin and the Darwinian Revolution*
> WW Norton, 1968, First edition
> New York, New York

Hitler, Adolf
> *Mein Kampf*
> Houghton Mifflin, 1971
> Boston, Massachusetts

Hooper, Judith
> *Of Moths and Men: The Untold Story of Science and the Peppered Moth*
> WW Norton, 2002, First edition
> New York, New York

Hunter, Cornelius G.
> *Darwin's God: Evolution and the Problem of Evil*
> Brazos Press (Baker), 2001
> Grand Rapids, Michigan

Bibliography

Johnson, Phillip E.
> *Darwin on Trial*
> InterVarsity Press, 1993, 2nd Edition
> Downers Grove, Illinois

Jones, Sydney
> *Hitler in Vienna: 1907-1913*
> Stein and Day, 1983
> New York, New York

Larson, Edward J.
> *Evolution: The Remarkable History of a Scientific Theory*
> Modern Library, 2004
> New York, New York

Lemonick, Michael D. & Dorfman, Andrea
> 'The 160,000-Year-Old Man'
> *Time*
> June 23, 2003
> Pages 56-58

Lewin, Roger

> *Bones of Contention: Controversies in the Search for Human Origins*
> Simon and Schuster, 1987
> New York, New York

Magee, Bryan

> *The Story of Philosophy: The Essential Guide to the History of Western Philosophy*
> DK Publishing, 1998, 1st American Edition
> New York, New York

Maiklem, Lara, Editor

> *DK Ultimate Visual Dictionary of Science*
> DK ADULT, 1998, 1st American Edition,
> United Kingdom

Martin, Jobe

> *The Evolution of a Creationist*
> Bible Discipleship Publishers, 2004, 6th Printing
> Rockwall, Texas

Bibliography

Morris, Henry M.

    The Long War Against God: The History and Impact of the Creation / Evolution Conflict
    Baker Books, 1989
    Grand Rapids, Michigan

Rennie, John,

    '15 Answers to Creationist Nonsense'
    www.ScientificAmerican.com
    June 18, 2002

Ridley, Matt

    Genome: The Autobiography of a Species in 23 Chapters
    Harper Perennial, 2000, First US edition
    New York, New York

Robinson, Tara R.

    Genetics for Dummies
    Wiley, 2005
    Hoboken, New Jersey

Sarfati, Jonathan
>   *Refuting Evolution 2*
>   Master Books, 2002
>   Green Forest, Arkansas

Smith, Wesley J.
>   *Forced Exit: The Slippery Slope from Assisted Suicide to Legalized Murder*
>   Times Books, 1997
>   New York, New York

Spetner, Lee M.
>   *Not By Chance! Shattering the Modern Theory of Evolution*
>   The Judaica Press, 1997
>   Brooklyn, New York

Stiffler, David
>   *Secret Museum of Mankind*
>   Gibbs Smith, 1999
>   Layton, Utah

Bibliography

Trefil, James

    1001 Things Everyone Should Know About Science

    Doubleday, 1992, 1st Edition

    New York, New York

Watson, James

    DNA: The Secret of Life

    Knopf, 2003

    New York, New York

Weikart, Richard

    From Darwin to Hitler: Evolutionary Ethics, Eugenics, and Racism in Germany

    Palgrave Macmillan, 2004

    New York, New York

Williams, William

    The Encyclopedia of Pseudoscience

    Facts on File, 2000

    New York, New York

Websites

http://news.bbc.co.uk/1/3013959.stm

www.biblebelievers.net

www.cstnet.com

www.encyclopedia.com

www.ScienceAgainstEvolution.com

www.TheOnion.com

www.law.umkc.edu/faculty/projects/ftrials/scopes

Index

A

A Century of Darwin   80
Aborigines   35, 60
Adaptation   19
Africa   35, 92
Agassiz, Louis   92
Agendascience   94
All Life is Struggle   56
America   57
American Biology Teacher   78
American Indian   57
American Museum
    of Natural History   113
Amino acids   28, 74
Analytical Chemistry   78
Angel of death   53
Angler fish   115
Antennaepedia   27
anthropologist   92
ape   51, 73, 91, 93
Archaeopteryx   17
Argon   82
Arts Council of Great Britain   75
Aryan   54, 60
Asian   57
astronauts   73, 93
Astronomer   77
Atheism   43, 53, 115
atheist   81
atheistic pseudoscience   71
atomic   84
Auschwitz   53
Australia   2, 105, 106
Australian Aborigines   105

Austria   5
Austrian   69
Austrian Pan-German party   49

B

backyard   85
bamboo   109
Barbules, feather   16
Barnett, S.A.   80
Barzun, Jacques   3, 113
BBC   75
Behe, Michael   24, 109
bicycle   85
Big Bang   84
Biochemistry   26
biogenesis   76
biologist   80
Biology   12, 46, 71, 94, 111, 114
biophysicist   88
bipedal   94
Birmingham   12
Birth defects   20
Black, Davidson   30
Blacks   40
Boeing 747   78
bogus theory   64
Bones of Contention   92
Borel, Emile   78
Botanist   42
Boyle, Charles   45
Boys, Don   51
British Museum of Natural History
    10, 111

British National
    History Museum   100
Burke, Edmund   119

C

calculus   85
Cambridge   80
Canadian Geological Survey   81
Cancer   26
Carbon 14   81, 82
Cassell Dictionary of Slang   51
cats   64
Caucasian   57, 58
Chamberlain, Houston Stewart   50
chance   78
chemistry   23, 80, 81, 94, 103, 118
chemists   74
Chimp   63, 93
Chimpanzee   63
Christian   85
Christianity   54
chromosomal abnormality   57
chromosome   63, 69, 71
Circular reasoning   20
Civic Biology   57
Clarke, Cyril   14
Cohen, I. L.   80
common ancestor   91, 93, 94, 99
common sense   84, 90
communism   113
Communist   113, 118
Comninellis, Nicholas   80, 82, 97, 98, 100
complex systems   71, 73
complexity   88
computer   74
Coon, Carleton   92
cross breeding   69
CSTNet.com   51
Currie, Kenneth L.   81

D

Darwin   46, 53
Darwin and the Darwinian Revolution   105
Darwin on Trial   33
Darwin, Charles   3, 9, 11, 88, 91, 105, 113, 114
Darwin, Marx, Wagner   113
Darwin's Black Box   26, 109
Darwin's Bulldog   51
Darwin's Demise   77, 98
Darwinian   98
Darwinism   92, 117
Darwin's God   117
Das Ausland   39, 40
Das Kapital   114
Dawson, Charles   100
DDT   66
de Beer, Gavin   100
'Delusion and Distortion'   96, 100
Desmond, Adrian   114
DNA   7, 61, 63, 64, 71, 89, 90, 98
Doolittle, Russell   26
Down Syndrome   58
Down, John Langdon   57
drug resistance   66
Dubois, Eugene   96, 97
Dusseldorf   98

Index

E

earth's age   115
Eddington, Arthur   86
E.D.M.   71
Edwin Conklin   51
Eldridge, Niles   7, 113
elites   59
Elmo   76
Engels, Friedrich   113
engineering   71, 115
engineers   64
England   100
Englishman   50
enlightenment   45
entropy   86
enzyme   78, 80
Eoanthropus dawsoni   101
ethnology   39
Eugene Dubois   96
Eugenics   1, 5, 46, 47, 48, 49, 59, 117
Europe   54, 57
euthanasia   49, 52, 106, 107
Evoligion   22, 64
Evolution   1, 9, 35, 47, 51, 53, 57, 58, 59, 61, 63, 64, 66, 70, 71, 76, 77, 79, 83, 84, 88, 90, 92, 93, 94, 97, 98, 100, 101, 103, 105, 106, 107, 109, 111, 113, 114, 115, 118
Evolution and Ethics   54
Evolution   99
Evolutionary Default Mode   71
Evolutionary math   90
evolutionist   81, 83
explosion   84

F

fairy tale   101
Faraday   34
feather   64
femur   96
Finches   9
Fischer, Klaus   59
fish   64, 65
Fisher, Ronald   81
Fix, William   78
Flat-earth   7
flat-earth theory   107
Fleishman, Albert   111
Forced Exit   106
forced sterilizations   106
Fossil   8, 111
fossil record   99
fossils   83
Fritsch, Theodor   48
From Darwin to Hitler   36
fruit fly   27

G

Galapagos Islands   3, 9
Galton, Francis   46
gene duplication   65
genealogy   46
genes   63, 79, 80
Genetic   20, 64, 66, 69, 70, 79, 80
genetic code   88
Genetics   8, 61, 69, 71
Genetics for Dummies   67
genocidal racism   43
genocide   58, 59, 60
Genome   61, 63
Genome   71

geologic   82
German   48, 53, 59, 97, 107
Germany   5, 48, 49, 54, 59, 98
Germany's savior   50
gibbon   98
Glendale College   74
Globalization   22
good in birth,   46
gorillas   64, 91
Goulay, Marcel   78
Gould, Stephen J.   33, 57, 83, 109
gradualism   83
Grant, Madison   47
Grasse, Pierre-Paul   65
gravity   31
Green, Jonathon   51
Gum   76

H

Haeckel, Ernst   34, 41, 42, 43, 61, 91, 100
Haeckel's Fraud's and Forgeries   58
Ham, Ken   106
Hamlet   74
Hanegraaff, Hank   17, 57, 86, 96
Hapsburg Lip   46
Hardison, Richard   74
Harvard   92, 97, 109, 114
Heather   76
Hellwald, Friedrich   40
Hereditary Genius   46
Hereditary Health Courts   56
Hereditary Illness   56
Himmelfarb, Gertrude   105
Hiroshima   84

Hitching, Francis   78
Hitler in Vienna, 1907-1913   37
Hitler, Adolf   50, 59, 91, 106, 107, 117
hoax   22, 96
hoaxmaster-in-chief   42
Hobart Museum   106
Holly   76
Holocaust   38, 43, 44, 48, 53, 56, 59, 60, 105, 106, 117
homeostasis   67
Hominid   21
hominids   93
Homo sapien   58
Hooper, Judith   13
hormone   80
Hoyle, Fred   77
human brain   67
human eye   73
Hunter, Cornelius   117
Huxley, Thomas   3, 5, 41, 51, 91, 94, 114
Huxley   114
hypothalamus   67

I

idiocy of atheism   90
igneous   82
illegitimate science   46
Indonesia   96
Inherit the Wind   107
insecticide   66
intellect   94
Intelligent Design   109, 115
intelligent falling   31
involuntary euthanasia   59

Index

J

Java Man   23, 58, 96, 97, 98
Jew   50, 53, 54, 56, 60
Johansson, David   97
Johnson, Phillip E.   33
Jones, Sydney J.   37

K

K-Ar   82, 83
Keith, Arthur   54
Kettlewell   13
Kosmos   42
Krause, Ernst   42

L

Lanz von Liebenfels, Jörg   49
Larson, Edward J.   105
Lectures on Man   41
legitimate science   103
Lehigh University   24
Lewin, Roger   93
Lewontin, Richard   97
Libby, William F.   81
logic   64, 80, 84, 94
London School of Economics   34
lower races   105
Luciferase   115
Luciferin   115
Lucy   97

M

Malay   57
Martin, Jobe   115
Martin, Robert   99
Marx, Karl   113

Marxist   113
math   77
'Mathematically Impossible'   71
mathematician   78
mathematics   22, 118
Medved, Michael   24
Mein Kampf   47, 50
Mendel, Gregor   69, 70
Mengele, Joseph   53
mentally inferior   41
metamorphic   82
Miller, Stanley   27
Missing link   30, 96, 97, 101, 106
Mistletoe   76
Mongolian   57, 58
Mongoloid Idiocy   57, 58
Mongoloid stage   58
Mongoloidism   57
monk   69
monkey   51, 74, 93
moral relativism   5, 43, 103
morality   94
Morris, Henry   44
moths   12
Mt. Ngauruhoe   83
Mt. St. Helens   83
mutant   14
mutation   80, 81
Mutations   65, 66, 70

N

Nagasaki   84
National History Museum   100
Natural Selection   11, 27, 56, 79, 80, 83, 88

Nature 78
Nazi   49, 52, 53, 55, 56, 117
Nazism   50, 56
Neanderthal   98
Nebraska Man   23, 96
Neck of the Giraffe   78
Negro   39, 57, 58
neo-Darwinian   89
New York Tribune   106
New York Zoological Society   47
New Zealand   83
Newton, Isaac   3, 45, 84, 85, 111
Nietzsche, Friedrich   5
Nobel Prize   81, 114
normalization of evolution   48
Not by Chance   89
nucleotide   63
Nuremberg   56

O

objective truth   117
Offspring   19
Ontogeny and Phylogeny   33
ontogeny recapitulates phylogeny   61
opposable thumb   109
orangutan   93
origin of life   84
ORP   61
Osborn, Henry Fairfield   29, 58
oxidizes   85

P

P.E   83
Paignton Zoo   75
paleontologist   58
panda   109
Pasteur, Louis   76, 77
Pasteurization   77
Pasteurize   77
Patterson, Colin   10, 18
PBS   79
pea plants   69
Peking man   30, 58, 96
Peschel, Oscar   39
Phillips, Mike   75
philosophical theory   118
philosophy   103
Phonysaurus Maximus   17
physician   49, 53
Physics   8, 23, 84, 85, 94, 103, 118
Piltdown   23
Piltdown Common   100
Piltdown man   58, 100, 101
Pithecanthropus erectus   96
Pitman, Michael   80
pituitary gland   67
Plowman, Amy   75
Political correctness   5
Popper, Karl Raimund   33
potassium-argon   82, 83
Prager   1
predator   70
prey   70
primates   75
primordial   27

Index

primordial ooze 89, 90, 93
Princeton University 51
Probability 8, 77, 111
pseudoscience 20, 31, 66, 84, 101, 107
Punctuated Equilibrium (P.E.) 23, 83, 113
Purdue University 53

R

Race 5, 57
racial extermination 41
racial genocide 54
racial inequality 49
racial purification 106
racial struggle 49
racism 36, 57, 92, 93
radioactive element 82
radiometric dating method 83
random chance 79, 88, 90
random mutations 66, 67
recapitulation 100
Recapitulation theory 57
Refuting Evolution 2 79
Rennie, John 18, 74
reptile 64
resistance 66
Ridley, Matt 71
Robinson, 67
Rockefeller Foundation 30
rocks 82, 83
Rolle, Friedrich 36
Rowan 76
Rudin, Ernst 55, 56

S

Sagan, Carl 81
Salisbury, Frank 78
Sarfati, Jonathan 79
Schmidt, Oscar 42
Schonerer, Georg von 50
ScienceAgainstEvolution.org 13, 63
Scientific Atheism 114
scientific method 34, 71
scientific racism 40
scientifically impossible 115
scientifically invalid 101
scientifically-invalid 118
ScientificAmerican.com 18, 74
Scopes 107
Scopes Monkey trial 57
second law of thermodynamics 84, 85
sedimentary 82
self-produce 86
Shakespeare, William 74
Simian 74, 93
'Similarity equals ancestry' 91, 101
Simon, Edward 53
skull cap 96
slavery 40
Smith, Wesley J. 106
social Darwinism 36, 47, 49, 50, 53
South America 105
species 80
speech 94

Spetner, Lee   65, 66, 89
spontaneous generation   76, 77, 115
squid   64
sterilization   47
Survival of the fittest   19, 37, 40

T

Tasmania   106
teeth   94
Tennessee   107
thalamus   67
The Bone Peddlers   78
The Handbook on the Jewish Question   48
The History of Culture   40
The Illustrated London News   29
The Lie: Evolution   105
The Logic of Scientific Discovery   34
The Long War Against God   44
The Miracle of Life   79
The Origin of Species   11, 59, 88, 107, 113
The Passing of the Great Race   47
The Secret Museum of Mankind   95
The Wonders of Life   42
theistic faith   58
TheOnion.com   31
Tierra del Fuego   105
Time magazine   35, 97
TOBEORNOTTOBE   74
tornado   78
transitions   111
Trefil, James   19, 85
typing monkey theory   73, 74

U

uber-race   60
unfit   47
United States   59
University of Chicago   27
University of Leipzig   40
University of Plymouth   75
University of Strassburg   41
USA Today   65

V

Victim of the Past   56
Vienna   48
Vienna, Austria   5
Vogt, Karl   41
volcano   83
Volta, Alessandro   34

W

W.H.A.L.E.   36
Waddington, C.H.   80
Wald, George   114
Watson, James D.   71
Watson, Lyell   99
Watt, James   3
weeds   49
Weikart, Richard   6, 36, 43, 49, 50, 52, 55, 59, 117
White, Joe   10, 80, 82, 97, 98, 100
willful ignorance   58
Woltman, Ludwig   37
Woodward, Arthur Smith   100
World War II   53

Z

Zoological Society of London   99
Zoologist   41
zoologists   97
Zuckerman, Solly   98